THE SHAMAN'S BODY

THE
SHAMAN'S BODY

▲ ▲ ▲

A New Shamanism
for Transforming
Health, Relationships, and
Community

ARNOLD MINDELL

HarperOne
An Imprint of HarperCollinsPublishers

HarperOne

HarperCollins books may be purchased for educational, business, or sales promotional use. For information, please e-mail the Special Markets Department at SPsales@harpercollins.com.

HarperCollins Web site: http://www.harpercollins.com

HarperCollins®, 📖®, and HarperOne™ are trademarks of HarperCollins Publishers.

FIRST HARPERCOLLINS PAPERBACK EDITION PUBLISHED IN 1993

Library of Congress Cataloging-in-Publication Data
Mindell, Arnold.
The shaman's body : a new shamanism for transforming health, relationships, and community / [Arnold Mindell].
    p. cm.
Includes bibliographical references.
ISBN 978–0–06–250655–9
1. Spiritual healing.   2. Shamanism.   I. Title.
BL65.M4M56   1993
291.1'4—dc20   92–56408

RRDPrintCode

CONTENTS

ACKNOWLEDGMENTS

I was shocked to hear that my old friend Professor Ben Thompson, from Antioch College, had died. I was even more surprised to learn that he had read chapter 14 of this work, "The Deathwalk," onto tape and then had it played back at his funeral. Ben's undying interest in this work gave me the necessary support I needed to dig it out of my files and publish it.

Thus, Ben Thompson inspired this new version of my work. By reading it at his own funeral, he reminded me that body sensations connected him to the dreamingbody, that essential part of ourselves that we experience as eternal.

I wish I had known when Ben was alive what I know now, after completing this book. The deathwalk, the struggle to be yourself against inner forces and outer rules, determines in part the length of personal life. The deathwalk is a contest with self-doubt and society over dropping into dreamtime. It is the precursor to a culture in which we create and dream together.

I felt honored by Ben many times as he encouraged some of his best students to study with me in Zurich, where I was working in the early 1970s as a training analyst at the Jung Institute. Best of all, he introduced me to Amy, my wife. Amy called Ben's wife that evening. She told us he had read "The Deathwalk" at his funeral.

But Ben and Amy were not the only people who helped me with this manuscript. I am also thankful to Julie Diamond, Jan Dworkin, Satya Gutenberg, Leslie Heizer, Robert King, Dawn Menken, Pearl and Carl Mindell, Elke Mueller, Cat Saunders, Max Schupbach, and Jytte Vikkelsoe. Thanks are especially due to Julie Diamond for some great conversations and for her editing. Leslie Heizer helped me with many of the details. Robert King drew many awesome sketches of the nagual, and Cat Saunders saved me from at least some of my worst errors.

Carlos Castaneda and don Juan, in *Journey to Ixtlan*, helped me connect the dreamingbody to psychotherapy. Joan Halifax enlightened me through her writings about core feminine elements of shamanism. I am especially thankful to Quest Publishers and to Jean Houston for her encouragement and idea of using the term *you* instead of *we* while addressing the reader. In this way, she indirectly asked me to identify with the shaman and teacher within myself. And, finally, my friend Michael Toms from New Dimensions Radio and senior editor at HarperSanFrancisco encouraged me to tell my own story about the occult practices mentioned in the last chapter of this book, which envisions a renewed culture based upon ancient shamanic ideas.

ARNOLD MINDELL

I lovingly express my deep indebtedness to those aboriginal healers and shamans and their communities in Africa, Australia, Canada, Japan, the United States, and India who renewed my interest in dreamtime by modeling lifestyles that are meaningful and awesome because of it. Their names are changed only in accordance with their wishes or to protect their privacy.

DESCRIPTION OF CONTENTS

At the core of everyday problems lies the dreaming-body, your most awesome experience, usually sensed only near death or in occult and shamanistic rituals. This new, exciting, and mythic side of life gives you greater control over your physical health and more insight into the nature of the world. *The Shaman's Body* encourages you to live the dreamingbody with others and to transform everyday reality into that special world where experience and answers to life's deepest questions appear.

This book is based upon personal experiences I have had with indigenous African, Native American, Australian aboriginal, and Indian Hindu healers and spiritual teachers from around the world and also upon my own seasoned practice of psychotherapy, conflict resolution, and shamanism. Exercises and methods are based upon a combination of modern psychology and ancient shamanistic practice.

Part I. *Developing a Double.* The first part of this book is devoted to practical methods for contacting your dreamingbody, becoming whole, and working with body and dream problems in order to develop a sense of self that is independent of society, time, and space.

1. *The Shaman's Body.* Why is it that you can sometimes find a quiet center in the midst of chaos and at other times seem almost to drown in the stream of everyday troubles as life pulls you about? The answer from psychology is that you fall into unsolved problems that must be worked out. In shamanism, the answer is different. Native healers say that a spirit influences your state of mind. The usefulness and thus the future of both psychology and shamanism depend upon the coming together of these two disciplines. I present innerwork exercises that update the most ancient human method of solving problems—that is, trance, the shaman's body experience.

2. *Shamanism and Processwork.* We speak of dreams, body experiences, and symptoms. But to really fathom these, we need to get into the stream from which they come, into the dreamingbody that creates them. To do this, I discuss various aspects of attention and differentiate our normal, everyday attention from a "second attention," which concentrates on irrational, unusual feelings and fantasies. By using the second attention, you can drop your normal self and sense the dreamingbody. In this way, certain problems get resolved in an irrational manner. The development of the second attention leads to a new kind of personal growth and, at the same time, follows ancient indigenous traditions. Here you find exercises around dream- and bodywork that lead to the dreamingbody.

3. *The Path of Knowledge.* Many rich paths lead to healing and creating a meaningful life. But a central aspect to all of

these is respect for irrational, powerful, and unknown forces that we cannot control. I share my experiences of working with these irrational forces from around the world. Exercises make these experiences realizable in the moment.

4. *First Lessons.* Ancient and general shamanistic teachings, like those of the Yaqui sorcerer don Juan, speak of gaining wisdom from synchronicities, that is, through listening to the environment. By taking unusual outer events seriously and even believing in your own lies, you come close to your personal myths. Otherwise, death itself must upset your notion of who you are and force you at gunpoint, so to speak, to give up and follow natural events. I tell stories from my practice, illustrating how death can be an adviser, and give exercises for practicing the lessons.

5. *The Hunter.* In all ancient native traditions, the solution to personal problems is closely connected to "power" and to following messages of the spirit in animals and plants and in your dreams and body. Without contact with this power, everyday life is not what it could be. But to find the power, you must become a hunter and learn certain minimal disciplines, some of which appear in the exercises at the end of this chapter.

6. *The Warrior.* Leaving everyday reality finally is not up to us but appears to be connected to a greater factor, which I have been calling the spirit. The move from our normal identity to the shaman's experience of the dreambody, the static picture that comes from bodily sensations or dream images, depends upon this spirit. But our capacity to go a step deeper awaits the development of the "second attention." Stories and exercises help to move this development forward in everyday life.

7. *The Ally.* The world of nonordinary reality inevitably involves confronting the most complex, the darkest, and the most terrifying thing we have tried to avoid throughout our lives, the inexplicable spirit "ally." But the very name of this

spirit figure indicates that it contains potentially valuable secrets. I focus on ally stories and how the demon appears in body problems, in depression, and in our most special abilities and worst troubles. Exercises help you to connect your problems with your allies.

8. *The Ally's Secret.* Ancient traditions and modern psychology advise that you either succumb to the ally or meet and wrestle with the spirit that threatens to possess you and ruin your body and relationships. In this chapter, I consider the meaning and nature of this confrontation and look at the connection of this being, your spirit, to your personal problems and culture. Methods and exercises help you to work with the ally and find its secret.

9. *The Double.* By meeting the ally and finding the mythic story behind your life, personal problems abate as you grow older. In this legendary time of maturity, you are simply who you are. Yet others may see you, from the outside, as if you had developed a double, a being independent of time and space, with parapsychological characteristics. This double is, for the one who experiences it, only a passing thought. The development that began with everyday problems and that led to your becoming a hunter and a warrior culminates in your becoming whole and congruent in every moment. Through stories from C. G. Jung and my own life, I try to make the double understandable, for it is the most mysterious aspect of all psychological and spiritual teachings. Exercises lead to experiments with the double in yourself and in your friends.

10. *The Path of Heart.* Parapsychological and occult tricks are not the heart of shamanism and are insufficient to make life worthwhile. In the light of near-death experiences, the only thing meaningful is whether life has had a certain, almost indefinable "heart" in it. The path of heart is something only the wisest part of you understands, something only elders still living in native settings seem to understand. To find this path today, you need a certain disciplined attention that

comes from the warrior's training. Methods for finding this path appear in the exercises, but the problem of how the individual path connects to the world is left open.

Part II. *Dreaming in the City.* If we change, the world around us must change as well. Otherwise, our development is crushed, or we suffer from the sense of inflation or isolation.

11. *Death or Sorcery.* The reality of dreambody experiences, of your dreams and body problems, birth, and death, implies that both the concepts of psychotherapy and the practice of indigenous shamanistic methods must change. I suggest a few such changes and imply new attitudes toward death and dying. I also provide exercises for you to use.

12. *Dreaming Together.* The town you live in is finally not a past you must avoid, but the source of a global spirit. I tell stories of experiences in Africa, Australia, India, and the United States with healers and wise people who have modeled incredible powers and love, the reality of living with the unknown. An African witch doctor couple were the greatest healers Amy and I have ever heard of. A mad priest from an Indian temple lived his dreamingbody and showed us the god Shiva. Australian aboriginal healers gave us a peak and very profound experience. In spite of its difficulties, this world is the most incredible one a human being could ever dream up. Exercises help you explore dreaming in the city.

13. *Phantoms and Real People.* Healers are ordinary and sometimes troubled people, too, as some of my stories about gurus and teachers show. All have had vast powers, but some could not live them fully in everyday life and find the path of heart. Yet all these mentors must be honored for the courage they have had to live the dreamingbody and transform life into magic. Exercises at the end of this chapter give a hint about how to honor your elders and their implicit life task by investigating their lineage.

14. *The Deathwalk.* Everyday life leads to deeper experiences than we would ever dream. But returning after these experiences to ordinary life is not always easy, for this mythic

return means nothing less than living the dreamingbody and the ancient, wondrous world of the shaman in the here and now, where such experiences often seem forbidden. What happens to you, the groups, and the world around you when you begin this return is simultaneously your personal death-walk and global evolution. If you repress your true self, you are threatened from within. If you live your self uncon-sciously and are possessed by it, you encounter troubles from without. In this chapter, I discuss the warrior's way of fruitful conflict with the inner and outer worlds. Such training may be necessary for you to survive the deathwalk and the en-counter with the spirit. Success or failure in this mythic pro-ject may determine not only the length of personal life, but also the sustainability of future culture. Exercises help you with the deathwalk.

15. *Dreamtime and Cultural Change.* What will happen to cultures in the future? Dreamtime will bring changes in our environment, community, and group life. Access to the dreamingbody creates a new feeling of enlightenment, in which connection to ourselves and to nature is coupled with influence in the evolution of history.

I

DEVELOPING
A DOUBLE

CHAPTER 1

THE SHAMAN'S BODY

ndigenous healers have taught me that the quality of life depends upon body sensations that are linked to dreams and the environment, to what I call the shaman's body. According to medicine people living in native settings around the world, and to mystical traditions, the shaman's dreamingbody, when accessed, is a source of health, personal growth, good relationships, and a sense of community.

The shaman's body (or dreamingbody) is a name for unusual experiences and altered states of consciousness that try to reach your everyday awareness through signals such as body symptoms and movement impulses, dreams, and messages from the environment.

The methods I present in this work for gaining access to the dreamingbody come from personal experiences I have had with Native American teachers in the United States and Canada, witch doctors in Kenya, Zen masters from Japan, healers from India, and aboriginal healers from the Northern Territory, Australia. In every instance, I have studied the effects of these shamanic experiences, developed related methods, which I discuss in this book, and tested those methods over the past twenty-five years in my therapeutic practice, extreme-state and chronic-body-symptom clinics, and international conferences.

According to warrior shamans, health problems, problems with relationships, and community difficulties are all aspects of your dreamingbody, peak life experiences that appear otherwise only near death, when you're on drugs, or in mystical rituals. Access to the dreambody is a key to your physical health and insight into the nature of the world. This book tries to make the dreambody less mysterious and more readily accessible so that you can use it to transform mundane reality into that special place where life feels deep and meaningful. It is based not only upon experiences with indigenous healers, but also upon my own background as a physicist, my earlier practice as a Jungian analyst, and my present work in process-oriented psychology and conflict resolution. The exercises and methods in the book combine modern psychology and ancient shamanistic practice and have been tested by thousands of people.

Yet this book is neither an academic study of shamanism nor a scientific proposal for a new psychotherapy. It is meant to be personal, and it recommends practical methods for gaining access to your own dreamingbody and ways to work on body problems and dreams. Finally, it explores the effects such innerwork or shamanism can have on the world.

Shamanism is meaningful for me because it illuminates not only personal experience, but also a cultural path toward a future, more sustainable world than our present one.

The Origins of Power

Elements of peak and shamanic experiences, such as prolonged trance states, spiritual awakenings, sudden healings, meetings with ghosts, and other paranormal events, are often foreshadowed by various types of inner experiences, or "callings," such as serious illness, near-death experiences, periods of near insanity, or "big" dreams of wise spirit figures. Mircea Eliade, in his seminal book, *Shamanism*, presents these callings as one aspect of shamanism worldwide.[1] Without them, the path to shamanism remains incomplete.

In the indigenous traditions in which I have taken part, shamans still teach about the importance of such callings. Some readers will remember Carlos Castaneda's don Juan figure, who says that the spirit determines how you identify yourself, whether you remain an average person, and whether and when you become a seer or a warrior, capable of sensing and following the signals and powers of the earth.[2]

The daughter of my Australian aboriginal healer told me that she prepares for and yet does not seek to learn witchcraft or to transform herself. She must wait as her ancestors did for her mentor, her father, until she reaches the age when such teaching is "allowed." She said she could not specify what age this would be, but she mentioned that her father was seventy-eight. He told me that he, too, had not sought to become a healer, but had waited until his parents taught him in their advanced old age, just before death. I shall talk further about the calling to become a shaman in a later chapter.

I have seen in my practice how many shamanic abilities appear when you stop doubting the reality of the spirit. In this moment, something in you transforms, and you develop a deep attention, a steady focus on irrational events. This basic shamanic tool is attention to the dreaming process. When your inner life calls and you stop doubting, a personal transformation begins. But all of this is not up to your will. You can work at transforming your personal life to make it more meaningful, but success with your attention is like a blessing that cannot be produced at will. Inner or outer teachers may spur you on, but it is finally up to the spirit to move your assemblage point—the way you identify, assemble, and conduct yourself, and your sense of reality.

Waiting for this special move is both sobering and challenging. Perhaps everyone has shamanic or intuitive abilities, yet few are able to use this capacity at will. Shamanic ability, like other talents, is not entirely at your disposal. You cannot simply determine when you are going to have important and healing experiences, though you can prepare for them through various practices, some of which I discuss in the following chapters.

The community in which one lives also plays a role in the shaman's calling. Of my many meetings with shamans, witch doctors, and healers, my most memorable healing experience was some years ago in Kenya. Other indigenous peoples have seemed more dissociated through contact with European or Western culture. In Africa, however, it became clear to me that the shaman or witch doctor cannot be studied independently of her or his relationship to the group, the tribe.

Our African shamans said that their power to heal is intimately connected to the needs and powers of the people and the environment in which they live. As a sign of honoring these powers, our African shaman healers not only worshiped the bush around them, but gave every child who crossed their path a penny, because, they explained, the children were the origins of their shamanic abilities. They said that when the children were happiest, shamanic medicine was most powerful.

Thus the power of the shaman's body is not only the shaman's, but is connected to the environment, the children, and the needs of everyone. This seems important to me at this point in time, at the beginning of a new century, because as shamanism is reborn and our interest in early indigenous cultures waxes as they wane, some modern students of shamanism think that they can develop shamanic ability simply through effort, interest, and study. But power belongs to the people and the world around us. As an Australian healer told me, we dream as individuals only because we are all dreaming together.

None of the indigenous shamans I have met identifies himself as such the whole day long. The word *shaman*, borrowed from Siberian culture, refers to one who works only part-time as a spiritual guide and healer. The shaman heals without identifying himself only as a healer, similar to a master in martial arts who fights without emotionally involving himself in a battle.

The shaman is independent of organized religion. The indigenous shaman always takes some form of psychic journey to the world of spirits to find what is missing in everyday life, traveling in her dreamingbody. Shamans are as individual as other people and, in my experience, do not seem to follow particular personality types. Some shamans focus mainly upon healing, while others are warrior shamans seeking the key to power and liberation.

There are medicine and warrior shamans, then. But all of us use our psychic powers at times to heal others or to find self-knowledge. Parapsychological and alternative medical powers appear regularly as part of the development of the shaman but are, in warrior traditions, considered secondary in importance to the overall development of the fluid, or flexible, seer, whose goal is to live on a spiritual path.

People with a calling to be a shaman must frequently apprentice themselves to a teacher. The gradually developing apprentice is in many ways similar to a person involved in psychotherapy. While many seek help from therapists, others often seem to be looking for spiritual or shamanic teachers. Thus, in a way, most psychotherapists who work with events that are far from ordinary consciousness—deep body experiences, trance—are seen in the dreams of their clients as practicing a form of shamanism.

Many clients in therapy portray themselves as the typically stubborn, blocked shaman's apprentice. You may feel that your "assemblage point," or identity, is often stuck in ordinary reality. You wonder why, if personal transformation is up to the spirit, this spirit usually waits until the end of life to open you up. Why is it so difficult to live the warrior's meaningful and wakeful life, sensing body impulses and following them, staying in touch with your dreamingbody?

Perhaps the spirit not only enlightens you, but also addicts you to ordinary reality. What other explanation can you give as to why you are more often focused upon everyday reality, doubting, repressing, and feeling embarrassed by your apprehension of the unknown? Why do you behave like everyone else when you are in a group, unable or unwilling to admit your access to dreams, the dreaming world, or the dreamingbody?

After all, being an ordinary person—is no fun. You take everything so seriously and personally. You always search for something meaningful to guide yourself with, hoping for enlightening dreams or experiences. As an ordinary person you suffer, are afraid of and expect the worst, and are oblivious to the power of the unknown. You are always defending your identity and your personal history. As a phantom, you constantly worry about how others judge you or what the future will bring. You neglect the impact of inexplicable forces, living life as if it were all up to you.

Shamanic Trainings

The Native American Yaqui way of knowledge and don Juan's concepts of the warrior and the double are eternal ideas that appear everywhere—not only in indigenous traditions, but in the dreams of people of all races, religions, and ages. Shamanism is an archetypal form of behavior that appears in you when you are faced with unsolvable problems. You may never have the chance to meet a shaman living in an indigenous tribe, but you can certainly have dreams and body impulses that recall witchcraft that is thousands of years old. Unusual dreams and the sense of the uncanny call you to remember the sorcerer, magician, and wise person in yourself.

You have probably had dreams or messages telling you to connect to your roots, to renew your earliest spiritual history, to journey to other worlds as men and women throughout history have done. Such dreams inspired Shamans to leave ordinary reality while remaining present for their communities. Many people today still feel impelled to experience drugs in order to find these altered states of consciousness. Others, suffering from chronic symptoms, return to shamanism as they discover the limits of Western medicine in reducing their suffering.

There are many types of shamanic training; some happen spontaneously within yourself when wise inner dream figures and body experiences guide you. Others are connected to spiritual or psychological teachers, traditions, and schools. In all, however, it is common to experience ordinary reality and its conventions, rules, and rituals as dangerous opponents. Consensus reality and social rules seem to repress signs from the unconscious. The reality most people follow seems to forbid you from investigating your hallucinations, aches and pains, and accidents.

The first worthy opponents whom you must overcome, therefore, often appear as those closest to you. The viewpoints of consensus reality, friends, and family—who may love you but be jealous of you—seem to be the greatest dangers to your progress. Patriarchal, conventional family systems and groups have a formidable power, like witchcraft, from which the shaman's apprentice must save herself. The warrior-to-be feels accused of disobeying cardinal social rules and of flirting with forbidden gods, with the spirit of nature.

Your warrior teachers may support these gods and open you to experiences of altered and dreamlike states of consciousness, which conflict with the ways of everyday life and friendships. Yet again and again, in spite of your teachers, you forget dreamtime; it seems to succumb to everyone else's reality. Sensing your dreams and managing the resulting social tensions requires the ability of a warrior on the path of heart.

Perhaps that is why, in spite of their heartfulness, shamans such as don Juan often appear as brutal, one-sided instructors, pushing but never quite succeeding in upsetting the stability of stubborn intellectual doings. In fact, the teachings of many authentic shamans are like don Juan's teachings; they occasionally feel like the hurtful slaps of scornful, insulted instructors, rather than the lessons of wise and detached masters.

Even when you consider that Native American teachings were developed in part to help individuals survive the imminent dangers of nomadic life, undue emphasis seems to be placed upon the development of power and warriorship. Is the battle the crucial thing, or is awareness? Without awareness, the best teacher is just another ordinary person possessed by a spirit and insisting that his way is the only way. Yet you cannot get around the warriorship phase, because at a certain moment, you begin to experience everyday events as a matter of life and death in which your opponents are both inner and outer.

You develop access to shamanic experience and the dreamingbody with the guidance from inner life, which shows your struggle to be a battle that only a warrior can survive. Outer instructors are helpful, for they give you the sense of companionship and community while turning you on to yourself. It may be that death is your wisest adviser. Some teachings, especially those from the Tibetan Bon religion and the Buddhist Tibetan Book of the Dead, point to the experience of death and the cessation of identity as the crucial instructor in life.[3]

Yet your ego does not die easily, and so you listen to subtle feelings and sensations only when they threaten to kill you. Mostly you tend to govern rather than to follow nature. You rely on doctors and therapists, counselors, priests, witch doctors, organizational developers, and even politicians, as if you wanted advocates against your own nature.

The shamanic path is different, for it is based upon sensing unpredictable events in yourself and the earth. The dreamtime spirit of the earth grounds, inspires, and teaches; it is an unfathomable being by itself. It is birdlike, a fish in the water, a racing cougar, the bear, the poisonous snake, the cloud above an alpine peak, the sun at dawn, a half moon. It is the sound of cars, the roar of a distant plane. It is what the aboriginal people of Australia, the oldest known human group on earth, call "Dreaming." These people, our earliest family, say that the events of this earth, our geology, and synchronicities are created by the earth's "dreamings."[4]

Indigenous tribal life may be fading out around the world as the next millennium begins. But the story of the shaman and the witch doctor is that of dreaming of an eternal vision that lives on in everyone and cannot be destroyed. You can kill an indigenous people, but no one has power over dreamtime. Shamanism itself is immortal. Perhaps that is why I heard one aborigine say that you can kill the kangaroo, but that is not serious, because kangaroo dreaming is indestructible.

Shamanism and Personal Growth

From the aboriginal viewpoint, modern psychotherapeutic techniques themselves are created or dreamed up by the earth spirit. Modern methods are helpful, even wonderful for many of us, much of the time. But today they need renewal, magic, and reconnection to ancient practices. They are too internal and do not deal with the transformation of communities and with the spirit of the environment. The development of therapy seems to have reached an impasse.

Our modern techniques often lack a sense of magic and do not address global issues such as racism, homophobia, women's rights, and poverty. Sigmund Freud, Carl (C. G.) Jung, Alfred Adler, Abraham (Abe) Maslow, Carl Rogers, Virginia Satir, Frederick (Fritz) Perls, and hundreds of others have brought us much. But therapy needs new blood to strengthen it so that it will work with political problems, abuse, revolution, and poverty, instead of focusing mainly upon people of the upper- and middle-income classes who have enough time, safety, and quiet for innerwork.

Let's look critically for a moment at where we are with therapy and spiritual traditions. Consider, for example, the development of my Jungian-based psychology, one I call process-oriented psychology, which provides tools for unfolding secrets encoded in dreams, body signals, and trance states. It is optimistic, and its tools and concepts allow me to work with people in comatose states in the same way as I would work with large organizations. Until this present study, however, I missed developmental concepts and practical tips about living with the natural environment and everyday life.

Taoism and the *I Ching* give me a sense of following processes through the use of divination. But Taoism is a mystery school and needs updating and practical methods to work with change in everyday life. Many speak of it today but cannot practice it. Buddhism's strength is in its potential openness; it is deep and heartfelt in its compassion for every aspect of human nature. But many misuse it to look down upon greed and violence instead of using it to discover how to deal with these feelings. Gestalt psychology is crucial to me for having brought out a dynamic view of the unconscious in the here and now, yet it needs updating in order to work with relationship, meditation, and groups. Jung is my spiritual mentor, yet Jungian psychology could use more body and more understanding of group life. Moreover, the analytical traditions do not work directly with the person in an altered state of consciousness, the central vehicle of shamanism. Transpersonal psychology emphasizes Eastern rituals and gives us hope and eternity through both Western and Eastern principles, and it needs more clinical reality. Finally, I love humanistic psychology, but where has its passion gone?

Masters in all of these schools and traditions have gone beyond their own methods and have had immense effects on the world. Yet many of these traditions and schools leave you impotent in dealing with large-group conflicts, racism, homophobia, and other aspects of ethnic, religious, and racial diversity.

This may be why Western psychotherapy has had only a small impact upon Africa, India, and Japan. Those at the growing edge of modern therapies realize that traditions from Asia, Africa, and India have the spiritual values, art, feeling, and movement that are missing in the West. Yet we all need more than the East or the West, and more than reverence for the past.

Even native indigenous shamanism of the healing type can be boring. The standard healer does all the work and requires little or nothing from the client. I, for one, shall never miss one aspect of indigenous life: the rigid roles in which everyone was placed. Men could do this, women had to do that, and only people from certain families could be shamans. Modern people want to be their own healers. The leadership and consciousness concentrated in the chief and the shaman must be shared in greater measure by all people in the future. There must be democracy at all levels.

Yet to go forward, it is helpful to look back. Therapy did not begin with Freud.

Modern sciences, allopathic medicine, and psychotherapy are only a couple of hundred years old, yet they are based upon alchemy and a shamanistic ancestry as old as the human race. Concepts like the "dreaming earth" are found among Australian aborigines, African shamans, Native American tribes, and all indigenous cultures going back as many as fifty thousand years.

Everything you do that is fun is based on shamanism. Dancing at discos until you go into a trance, screaming yourself into a frenzy at a ball game or music festival, running until you are in an altered state of consciousness: All are shamanic. And what about fundamentalism and the passion for god? Don't forget that the oldest churches in modern Europe were built upon ancient power sites. We tend not only to build over our past and injure native people, but also to deny our own magic and belief in the unknown and to act like rationalists, as if we had created the world.

Western psychotherapy, without reference to ancient world history, tends to be a mostly white, middle-class dream with as much air as earth. It is a useful dream, but it misses the eccentric nature of the shaman, love for community, and a culture in which self-knowledge is based on powerful altered states of consciousness.

As serious doubts about our present world culture arise, we find ourselves looking critically at our sciences, medicine, and culture. None of these was created with the idea of sustainability, with the sense that whatever we do ruins or makes possible life for the future. New steps need to be made to reflect the uncanny world of the shamans and their sense of living in harmony with nature; yet these steps also must satisfy our needs for science, group life, trouble, and spirituality.

The Path of This Book

Until now, my identity as a psychotherapist has made me hesitate at the point of the spirit world and living the dreamingbody for fear of being misunderstood. However, my outer and inner lives can no longer tolerate such one-sidedness. After having observed how colonial Western politics have literally decimated millions of aboriginal people in Africa, Australia, North America, and India, and after having realized how the native peoples of Japan, China, Hawaii, and Alaska have been oppressed and murdered, silence is no longer an option for me. The political reality of aboriginal peoples today amounts to lack of civil rights. These peoples are not allowed their religious beliefs. Nations that claim to be democratic, including the United States, occupy and destroy what remains of aboriginal power spots, implying that aboriginal religious groups that worship the earth are not as important as religious groups that require concrete buildings in which to worship.[5]

In a way, this book is a test for me, a kind of deathwalk. Like the figure who faces a jury of outer and inner forces, a story I will tell in chapter 14, I must congruently explain the necessity for living on the border between theoretical physics, shamanism, and psychology—or be shot down by inner-spirit critics for hesitating, or by the world of psychotherapy for becoming an irrational mystic. I must drop my personal history and reputation to write this book.

Shamanistic teachings are life-and-death matters these days. I think of the many native teachers I have known who have had their lives threatened for speaking about ancient ways to nonnative peoples. The aboriginal daughter of our Australian healers explained the dangers involved. While painting the back of a two-hundred-year-old turtle shell near her shanty, she said that her father had told her that the experiences we had with him could be written about but not discussed with others. She meant that the power of ancient dream- and bodywork must not be reduced through analysis, but it wants to be known to all. It is as if dreamtime were calling us today to remind us of the presence of the past; yet this dreamtime is an experience that may never be fully comprehensible in our everyday languages.

You must wait for life to provoke and even to force you, sooner or later, to experience the dreamingbody. The dreamingbody lies hidden beneath our everyday problems, relationships, family and group struggles, problems of children and adults, crises of love, midlife depressions, retirement, and near-death experiences. And everyone will, of course, one day die.

Whether fate is called acute or chronic illness, academic or business failure, sexual hang-up, insanity, suicide, or secret love affair, the pattern for living the dreamingbody hovers in the background as the antidote to pain. Our biggest problems seem to be meant to interrupt life and awaken us to our total capacity, warriorship, and death, to end our earlier personality and find the path of heart.

Processwork and Dreamtime

While waiting for this book to mature over the past thirty years, while slowly growing into aspects of eldership, I have improved my practice of what I have been calling psychotherapy. I have studied physical illness and near-death situations, addictions, extreme states, street people, group and international problems, children, Alzheimer's victims—

even shamans. Everything I have done seems to circle around dreamtime.

Native American concepts and concepts of Australian aborigines have had a powerful influence on my work, as can be seen in the names of my books—*Dreambody: The Body's Role in Revealing the Self; Working with the Dreaming Body; River's Way: The Process Science of the Dreambody; The Dreambody in Relationships; The Year I: Global Process Work with Planetary Tensions;* and *Inner Dreambodywork: Working on Yourself Alone.* My original name for what is now called process-oriented psychology was dreambodywork, emphasizing the connection between the world of dreams and the experiences of the body.

As I wrote this book, I was constantly plagued by new questions and sought the answers to perennial problems. What does living the dreambody imply, not only for yourself when you have powerful peak experiences through therapeutic and shamanistic methods, but for everyone, for the future of life on earth? In what ways does the dreambody experience go on after death? Finally, am I sufficiently developed to write this book? Am I clear about myself or old enough to be critical of therapy and shamanism?

EXERCISES

1. Recall a time when you were working with yourself. Perhaps you were meditating or doing dreamwork or bodywork, engaging in spiritual ritual or some innerwork procedure, and suddenly you found that you were having a good "trip," that is, you were journeying in other dimensions, into altered states of consciousness. Such a trip is a central element of shamanism, and such journeys may be callings to be a shaman. If you have not had such an experience, this book may make such experiences more available to you.

2. Other experiences that may be callings to learn more about shamanism are chronic illness, feelings of insanity, prolonged dreamy states, or the appearance of wise dream teachers

in dreams or waking states. Recall any such experiences now. Remember the unusual moods they may have produced in you.

3. Experiment with "assembling," that is, identifying yourself in different ways. For a moment, see yourself as a person who always follows the dreaming process. Don't worry about how to define this process; simply let your imagination lead you here. Follow these earlier "callings" in your imagination as if they were a process trying to dream you into a certain state and not simply a symptom of your being troubled. What state have these early "dreamings" been aiming at?

4. Now see yourself on a good "trip," or imagine an inner wise figure who can support special states or experiences. Take a moment and connect to these imaginations, figures, methods, and trips.

5. Notice if your inner experience or teacher has some type of message for you. Experiment with sensing this message and taking it seriously.

6. Imagine living this message in your life, relationships, and work. Imagine any changes you must make in your everyday life.

CHAPTER 2

SHAMANISM
AND
PROCESSWORK

Healers and helpers use many methods and names for healing and for experiences of well-being: the Tao, God, the Way, the here and now, chance, fate, Kismet, Kronos, the unconscious, synchronicity, individuation, enlightenment, and so on. Process-oriented psychology, or processwork, refers to such ultimate experiences as living the dreamingbody. Shamans refer to the dreamingbody in terms of a sense of power.

The dreamingbody answers the perennial question, How do you live in a way that feels balanced yet exciting, peaceful yet fun, satisfying yet terrifying? If you try to control or manipulate your energy, you end up feeling ill or dead. If you follow your body's sensations, you feel more completely here, as if you are really living and creating life. Following sensations such as aches, pains, and dizziness means living your dreamingbody.

Modern ideas about dreams and dreaming go back to ancient mythology. Celestial ascents and descents to the underworld involving the dreamingbody are basic to shamanism and may be our oldest and most widespread human spiritual experience.

Like all shamanic teachings, dreambody concepts are comprehended best through direct body experience. Without self-evident body experience, the teachings sound like attractive mysteries that our thinking misinterprets as tales about other realities, metaphors about drug trips, or unreal projections of the unconscious.

To get to the experience of the dreamingbody, I work first with dreams and body experiences. In following chapters, I try to illuminate some of the alterations in worldviews that may be necessary to maintain awareness of the dreamingbody.

Dream and Body Snapshots

If you think about what happened to you last night while you were sleeping, you may remember body feelings, dreams, or both. As you recall dreams, you take them out of the sleeping and dreaming context in which they occurred and inadvertently change them. Most modern dreamwork procedures deal with dreams outside of their original context.

Out of context, dreams are fragmented stories, pictures that you can no longer quite remember from ongoing experiences. They are like momentary and incomplete snapshots of a river, so to speak. Shamanic experiences, however, come mainly from the streaming river itself. The term "process" in "processwork" refers to the shamanistic act of journeying directly with the river. Processwork for a given individual can also be ordinary therapy, since it deals with dreams as snapshots of another reality.

ARNOLD MINDELL

Seen from the viewpoint of the river, dream reports from the night are pictures of deep processes that have occurred. Remembered dreams are unconscious aspects of yourself frozen into time. They are like a photo album of an awesome trip.

Body sensations can be similar to dreams. If you talk about them, they, too, become snapshots of the stream of experiences. If you say that you are tired or have a sore throat, for example, you are reporting on momentary body or proprioceptive feelings. Although these feelings may begin as fatigue or a sore throat, if you get closer to and into them—if you consciously immerse yourself and climb into them—they soon flow on and evolve as a dreaming process.

The Dreamingbody

The stream of experiences known as dreamingbody not only occurs at night but seems to be always happening to you. One of the shaman's main tasks is to gain access to the dreaming process during the day. The dreams that you recall are interesting, but they are no substitute for access to the dreaming process itself. Likewise, medical, anatomical, and physiological descriptions of your body are not substitutes for your experience of the dreamingbody.

Most of the time, you focus on only those body sensations that go along with your daily program. You repress everything else. You stay close to home and avoid the uncanny, natural environment, fearing it as if it were a wilderness area. You think the body is ill when it becomes troublesome, and you fail to realize that it is trying to dream, to communicate messages and create movements beyond your expectations.

For example, one of my clients dreamed that he had died. In this dream, he came out of his body but was amazed to still be awake. Instead of working on this dream, we followed his momentary body experience, which he described as a sense of being tired. When he focused on this experience, the fatigue transformed into relaxation and a sense of letting go.

He then felt and followed spontaneous shaking movements, which began in his knees, and suddenly we were in the midst of something that he could no longer explain. He felt that these spontaneous movements were propelling him to walk about in a strange, jittery, gawky manner. Suddenly he stopped and said with surprise that he felt that dead spirits were moving him.

Now he was living his dreamingbody. His body was moving as if he were being dreamed. His death or spirit had freed itself from his old body and his personal identity. He was moving as if he were dead. But something new was animating him, entering his body in order to direct it the way it wanted to go. He was not dead at all, but more fully alive then ever before.

Though this dream and body experience belongs to a particular individual, it shows an important connection. If you take body snapshots, momentary body experiences or signals, and use them as invitations to the unknown—if you let them evolve and unfold—they mirror recent dreams and become the dreamingbody.

This is an empirical experience that anyone can test: Dreams are snapshots of body experiences that are trying to happen, and body experiences mirror dreams. I call this symmetrical connection between snapshots of dreams and the body the "dreambody."

Together with other processworkers, I have been able to test the dreambody connection around the world with many thousands of people of all ages and in all conditions. We have found that the dreamingbody experience is found in everyone: people in Nairobi, African warriors on the desert, the Japanese, Australian aborigines, Indians, Europeans, people from the Americas, Russians, and so on.

While my discovery of the dreambody has developed from the connection between dreams and the body, the concept has evolved, and I have focused upon the dreaming process in many branches of experience, with couples, groups, and individuals in many states of consciousness. The concept is also useful for people who are ill or in near-death situations.

Dreambodywork, or process-oriented psychology applied to the body, is a matter of sensing your body sensations and allowing them to direct the way in which you live. Following the dreamingbody is a most important task. It is the channel for what some call the "dream maker" and what others refer to as the "spirit," or the unconscious. Native Australians call it "dreamtime." Shamans refer to it as "becoming a warrior on the path of heart."

Paying Attention and Focusing

The training that you need to live the dreamingbody can be found in shamanic lessons, which I shall describe in the following chapters. Before I begin that, however, I will describe exactly where I think such lessons fit into the general topic of awareness and attention.

Everyone knows the idea of paying attention; we all tell each other to pay attention. Without loving attention as a child, you can die. As a child, you are trained to pay attention to your parents and teachers and to the everyday doings of the world. Meditators train themselves to pay attention to the flux of inner experiences, images, and body sensations. Teachers and therapists are trained to pay attention to students and clients. Lovers pay attention to one another. Yet we often feel that we have not gotten *enough* attention.

Shamans must pay attention to unusual events in themselves, their clients, and the environment. Since a shaman must be able to lead a normal everyday life, she also develops attention to everyday reality, a focus that don Juan calls the "first attention." But the shaman must develop the attention for unusual processes—namely, the "second attention," which perceives the dreaming process.

I use don Juan's terms in a special manner. When you focus on someone with your first attention, you perceive the meaning of what they are saying. With the second attention, however, you notice aspects of their living dreaming, which I shall describe in the next section.

As the receiver of attention, you may know what it is like to be listened to or understood through someone's first attention. But it can be even more fulfilling to be seen by someone giving you the second attention.

The many kinds of shamans and apprentices seem to divide up mostly into medicine and warrior, or spiritual, shamans and seekers. Medicine shamans develop their second attention for healing and helping others; most use their abilities for their clients without requiring the same awareness from the clients. This is perhaps why shamanism is so widely applicable; like modern medicine, it does not always require special consciousness from the recipient.

Warrior shamans develop their skills for self-knowledge, while medicine shamans focus mainly on therapeutic effects. In contrast to shamanism in general, the processworker shares responsibility for perceiving special states of consciousness with clients and tries to encourage them to develop their own second attention whenever possible.

In processwork, "following the process" depends on the client's state of awareness as much as it does on the therapist's awareness. Both need to develop their second attention. I will not describe processwork further, since I have done so elsewhere in my writings, and since I want to update processwork by reference to shamanism. Nor will I analyze or explain shamanism or try to prove why or whether it works. I am more interested in what it teaches us about working with ourselves and our present world situation.

My experiences with near-death situations show me that most people drop their first attention, fall into the second one, and enter the dreamingbody near the end of life. Near death, we all experience our dreams as body experiences and seem to move with subtle, unpredictable inner and outer events. Death, the inevitable outcome for each individual, gives us perspective on our everyday lives.

Thus, the first attention is the awareness needed to accomplish goals, to do your daily work, to appear the way you want to appear. The second attention focuses upon things you normally neglect, upon external and internal, subjective, irrational experiences. The second attention is the key to the world of dreaming, the unconscious and dreamlike movements, the accidents and slips of the tongue that happen all day long.

In order to lead a normal life, you feel that you must kill, repress, or heal some of these signals and symptoms if they are disturbing, especially if you interpret them as diseases to be overcome. In special states of consciousness—while dreaming, in a coma, in creative dance, in ecstasy, during sports or loving—you slip into the second attention, however, and begin to live the dreamingbody. During psychoticlike episodes—that is, in extreme states of consciousness, such as hallucinations or multiple personalities—the dreaming process may overwhelm you.

Your job as warrior is to follow, feel, and process these sensations and to wander along paths similar to those of your nighttime dreams. The dreamingbody experience makes you feel whole and creative. When you are in the dreamingbody, you are neither awake nor dreaming, neither in nor out of your body.

From the outside, your dreamingbody experience may seem unusual to others; it makes you do unpredictable things, and others think you may be on drugs or having a peak experience. From the inside, however, you experience familiar yet incomprehensible sensations and motions. When you let these unfold, you feel connected to something essential; you become your whole self, independent of space, time, and the world.

Double Signals

When you use your first attention, you focus on your "primary process," your normal identity, and rarely develop the second attention necessary to focus upon "secondary processes," the dreamlike events that transpire, such as accidents, slips of the tongue, and synchronicities. Hence, these secondary processes continuously happen to you without your involvement. Yet people around you notice them. You emit them as double signals. They are what make you amazing, impossible, incomprehensible, powerful, and troubled.

Double signals are unintended messages, your living unconscious, the dreamingbody as it is experienced in relationships. Some of these signals are seen and heard, for instance, in the unconscious manner in which you walk and in the tone you use in speaking. But you can also communicate with others in a manner outside the laws of physics. That is why people can sense your double signals and dreaming process at a distance and why shamans can heal clients who live far away.

You need to understand at least the concepts of primary and secondary processes and the first and second attentions in order to deal with the unusual and altered states of consciousness that shamans and sorcerers experience. Today, most therapists realize that important experiences and transformations do not happen fully without access to these states. You need the ideas of primary and secondary processes to help you gain access to dreamtime.

The ideas of the ego, the conscious, and the unconscious are useful for dealing with people who remain in normal states of consciousness. But we need different concepts for dealing with those in comatose states, having psychotic episodes, or in other extreme states of consciousness such as those a shaman may experience.

I remember, for example, a student who got stuck on a drug experience years ago in Switzerland and was brought to me in the midst of a frightening delirium. He stumbled around my room, screaming that the walls of my office were moving. When he touched them, he said, they bent. He cried because he had hurt them by touching them so roughly. The longer this went on, the more terrified he became.

This experience would have been sufficiently meaningful left to itself. But he wanted me to help him because of the terror he experienced. He was on the verge of having a "bad trip." For me to work with him in such a state, the concepts of ego, conscious, and unconscious were not useful. Instead, I thought of the wall as a secondary process with which he did not identify and asked him to believe in the wall, to feel and look at it.

"Focus your attention upon it!" I yelled. "Look at it!" I had no idea what would happen when he used his second attention. Immediately, the moving wall turned into a wave on which he saw himself riding. I encouraged him to show me the wave in movement, to move as he saw the wave moving. He stood and made magnificent wavelike dance movements, surfing his visionary ocean as the waves crashed onto the beach.

Suddenly he stopped, looked at me soberly, and said, "Arny, I am just too rigid in my studies!" His delirium abated as he became excited about new directions in his studies. He needed more flexibility in his life. In this experience, the student had identified himself to begin with as a sensitive person in touch with the pain of matter. While some therapies traditionally focus on strengthening the ego—in this case, the young man's personal history as a student—processwork, like Gestalt and Eastern traditions, focuses upon awareness. The basic idea is that identity is a momentary process, and the way you identify yourself in the moment is as a "primary process" that changes all the time.

The focus in processwork and shamanism is not upon developing the ego further but rather upon developing awareness of change. Again, being aware means paying attention, developing the first attention to focus on momentary reality and the second to perceive altered states of consciousness. The goal of the warrior is to develop the second attention, for this leads to living the dreamingbody and finding the path of heart.

Developmental Ideas

Psychology helps you with your problems; it goes to the door of the other world, waits for something to come through, and uses that something. But what happens when you solve some of your problems and become interested in what lies beyond, when you are tempted to go through that door and continue into the unknown?

Even though you will always have personal problems, your own aging process provokes questions about the nature of other worlds. Many people are content to stay on this side of the door until the last minute. But the question about other worlds will become more intense in the future. As the natural environment suffers continued abuse and the wilderness becomes more limited, you shall have to make more out of less, and to do this you will need the second attention.

Shamanic ideas inform us about the development you undergo as you encounter the dreaming world. Mircea Eliade has discussed typical stages of becoming a shaman, stages such as the quest for magical power, initiatory illness and dreams, methods for searching for the soul, and secret rituals. Many apprentices called upon to move into the unknown go through developmental stages and discover themselves becoming hunters, sorcerers, seers, warriors, people on the path of heart, and so on.

The hunter is a person who understands reality and notices when unusual events are about to happen. The individuation process later creates the warrior, a step you experience at certain times of heightened awareness and near the end of life. As a warrior, you use your second attention, flexibly step out of time, and leave the cycle of problems behind. You get off the wheel of life and death and become your whole self by flowing with experiences. Final steps are beyond technique and deal with learning to follow the path of heart. Among Native Americans, this is sometimes called the "red path"; it is the feeling basis to our personal growth, the heartfelt sense of being or not being on the right track. Western ideas about individuation seem dry without this sense of the heart and the specialness of the quest.

Shamans such as don Juan, who live either in indigenous conditions or in the midst of a warrior group, teach about different stages in personal development through living in nature. Their teaching submerges us in a dimension of life that has become foreign to many people today. This dimension is the dreaming earth, the power of the natural environment our species is close to ruining.

Not only are we in danger of losing our rainforests and ruining our natural environment, we have forgotten our second attention, which senses the magic of the world around us. We are not only killing the environment, we are suffering simultaneously from self-abuse, by negating our own incredible potential. Those who develop a second attention and a dreamingbody feel more secure, freer from life and death, and able to preserve the magic of both personal life and the environment.

EXERCISES

1. Think of a dream that you have had recently. Note the feeling that was most memorable in the dream. In which part of the dream was this feeling?

2. Now put the dream aside, so to speak, and note what sort of body experience you are feeling in the moment.

3. You may be having two experiences, one common to you and one unknown. Try to isolate the less common body experience, the one that is unknown, undesirable, or difficult. Take time to perceive it.

4. Using your second attention, focus upon this lesser known body experience. Let this experience evolve. Get into it; feel it first. Then experiment with expressing this feeling with your hand. Let your hand move a little. Exaggerate your motion until you find out where it is going.

5. If the resulting experience reminds you in some way of a part of your dream, you may now understand your dream better. This movement experience mirrors the feeling in the dream and is a momentary experience of your dreamingbody.

6. Swing back and forth between paying attention to your normal body experience and your normal identity and paying attention to this new experience found in your dreamingbody. Practice going in and out of your dreamingbody.

CHAPTER 3

THE
OF
KNOWLEDGE

There are many paths to the top of the
mountain. Once you are there, all may look
the same. When you are at the bottom,
however, the differences between teachers
and spiritual paths are crucial, because some apply
and some do not apply to your changing moods and
lifestyles. The shaman's path, for example, becomes
important when you seek encouragement for entering altered states of consciousness. Jung's path is
crucial if you must understand dreams and symbols
of the path. Processwork is useful if you must work
with or live altered states in everyday reality. The
transpersonal path is necessary to validate spiritual

31

experience. The Zen path happens when living in the moment is the way to detachment.

Personal change and transformation go by many names, each one stressing a different characteristic of psychospiritual growth. For example, in parts of the subcontinent of India, the irrational and loving interactions between a guru and a disciple guide the development of a subtle dreamingbody. In Taoism, developing a dreamingbody depends upon adjusting to the cyclical flow of Yin and Yang, becoming like a cloud that rains and pays no attention to the boundaries between two cities.

The various Buddhist processes of personal growth are connected to increasing awareness, to discovering or creating a fair observer, i.e., a detached point of view. Enlightenment happens spontaneously and cannot be obtained through will power alone. In Zen, enlightenment appears as a special attitude toward life. One of our Japanese Zen masters, Keido Fukushima of the Tofukuji Monastery in Kyoto, teaches that "every day is a fine day," meaning that even the most impossible fate is somehow acceptable with the right attitude.

In Cabalistic Judaism, personal development is likened to a magical tree that takes root, reaches for the sky, and develops all the branches of our powers. In alchemy, people are seen as unrefined mixtures of opposites. Growing means cooking and transforming, with a vessel for conflict that transforms and transmutes our natures.

Enlightenment and development in Western psychotherapy are equally as wide-ranging. In the following synopsis, I offer only brief generalizations of complex systems of therapy. In parts of the world where European languages are spoken, Freudian psychoanalysts focus upon the awareness of repressed feelings. Issues of sex, death, and self-esteem are linked to childhood experience. Adler demonstrated how personal growth leads through the drive for power and connected inner life to social roles. Gestalt therapy reminds us of the presence of the here and now. Body therapists identify personal growth in terms of physical sensations, such as relaxation or well-being. Maslow and transpersonal psychology connect personal growth with detachment from strong experience, compassion for others, and self-actualization.

According to Jung, you are concerned in the first half of life with adapting to society. In the second half, you live out universal and spiritual roles. Individuation involves making the unconscious conscious. This process happens continuously, sometimes with awareness of growth, other times without it. By observing dream series over long periods of time, Jung hypothesized that personality slowly oscillates around the self, the complete person. Jung called the lifelong process of psychological maturation and attainment of self-knowledge "individuation." It is the central, guiding drive in life, the result both of growing older and wiser and of biological, psychological, and environmental evolution.

Despite its overwhelming importance, we know little about the process of personal growth. We know about its symbols, such as the circle, spiral, and mandala, but not much about its effects upon our relationships, our body, or our environment. How does the body change in response to increasing wisdom? What determines the length of life? Why is a person's life sometimes violently terminated at an early age? We don't know how personal growth connects to world evolution, and we are only beginning to learn how to work with extreme mental and physical illnesses.

We study projection, and we all search for someone to show us the way and parent our growth. Yet we care too little about apprenticeship, the necessary and loving relationship between the learner and the learning facilitator.

Many psychotherapies and spiritual traditions could profit from the shamanistic viewpoint about development. Individuation, detachment, and self-actualization are important concepts referring mainly to behavior in ordinary reality. If what happens at the very end of life is any measure of your final goal, you need to consider the dreamingbody and altered states of consciousness in connection with personal development. The shaman works at lucid dreaming, stalking visions, following body sensations, and worshiping nature, promoting not only personal growth but environmental awareness and a sense of community. As in Tibetan and Egyptian traditions, the shaman works on the afterlife experience, so to speak—on events that happen after you gain freedom from your identity, your personal history.

Most paths attempt to transform our personal identity. A good therapist will look like a Jungian, Freudian, dancer, storyteller, shaman, analyst, teacher, or idiot, depending upon the situation. In a process-oriented view of personal growth, the individual not only changes her behavior but expands her attention. Maturation means paying attention both to events that support your identity and to the disavowed aspects of life—to which you do not usually pay attention—that disturb.

With innerwork, good luck, and study, this growth process means an increased ability to use both your attention and your awareness as they gradually detach from your self. From a detached viewpoint, you are, for moments, at least, connected neither to your old identity nor to new things that arise within you. The moment you identify yourself as being aware of the flow of life and also as being a part of the flow, you have a peak and meaningful experience. Many people describe this state in terms of nothingness—that is, you know that you are at any one moment any one of your different parts and yet none at all.

This bare outline of the process of personal growth accords in many respects with spiritual traditions that do not stress the psychology of the ego or of consciousness. The manner in which this growth proceeds depends entirely upon the individual. Thus you may describe your work in terms of the discovery of the unconscious or in terms of the taming of the serpent, the Kundalini. Change comes sometimes from an unsolvable problem or koan, sometimes from a group interaction, sometimes from a body experience. Processwork does not focus on who you are or might become but on what you notice. As in Buddhist traditions, you meet one of its goals the moment you identify yourself as the facilitator of events, in contrast to being one of the events themselves.

Inexplicable Forces

The process view has much in common with Castaneda's *Eagle's Gift*. Don Juan tells the warriors' myth in which the eagle has granted every human being the chance for eternity, and every living thing has the chance to "avoid the summons to die" by perpetuating the "flame of awareness." In this beautiful and moving tale about the struggle for liberation, developing means disciplining awareness, differentiating attention, and becoming a person of knowledge. But what motivates you to take this path?

Eliade points out that the shaman's path is a forced one; people are driven to it through illness, hereditary predisposition, dreams, magic, and bodily dismemberment.[1] All sorts of awesome activities are part of the shaman's path. They terrify him and vivify his way. Seeing spirits, hearing secret languages, and experiencing indescribable events—including taking the road of the dead—fill his life. It is not surprising to hear in the modern don Juan story of shamanic teaching that this path to awareness is complex, a "forced" battle in which the unknown spurs you.[2]

Because you are always trying to repress or avoid something, or to fight something, it is not surprising that the shamanic path is called the warrior's way. Either you are the unknowing victim of some other person or force, or you are attempting a heroic feat, preparing to meet inexplicable forces that are forever greater and more powerful than you are. While some choose to vacation rather than to meet these forces, the proverbial teacher explains that these inexplicable forces come to you whether you are ready for them or not. You must encounter them, succumb to them by becoming dissociated, or make them your allies.

The shaman's path is a lifelong struggle with the unknown. It is full of tension, because you are constantly confronted with new aspects of reality that lie just beyond your ever-increasing ability to deal with and integrate them. Pressing and problematic dreams, insufferable body problems, severe relationship crises, addictions, untenable moods, and aspects of fate provoke you to awaken and fight for your life. Life seems to attack you as an opponent, perhaps because you disavow it. You see the disagreeable or unknown as an aspect of reality that does not belong to you.

You think, "I am this and not that. I will never be like that." You think everything dreamlike comes from another reality. As you open up to new aspects of life, the unknown becomes more familiar and appears to be what is trying to happen in the moment. But with each insight, new and apparently incomprehensible situations arise, spurring you on or hindering you. You always try to determine instead of to follow fate.

The shamanic teacher understands these conflicting aspects of fate not as opponents that must be overcome but as potential and possibly the most powerful allies. Inexplicable forces are just that. Whether they are monsters or divinities, body problems, or world or relationship troubles, they challenge you to expand your identity and to accept them as the magic carpet to renewal. One aspect of the powers that drive you may be named; the other is indescribable, according to chapter 1 of the *Tao Te Ching*.

Australian aborigines speak of power similarly. In one story, a man says, "My father said . . . 'My boy, Look. Your Dreaming is there. It is a big thing; you must never let it go [pass by]. . . . Something is there; we do not know what; something . . . like engine, like power, plenty of power; it does hard work: it 'pushes.' "[3]

Native teachers try to awaken you to the power of the unknown, to this "something," this enginelike power and the fact that it works. Yet its exact nature is difficult to explain. In all traditions, the central means of working with opposing forces is through respect for the inexplicable nature of power.

Whereas many psychological and spiritual systems propose explaining and avoiding blocks, shamans claim that they contain "power" that only partly belongs to you. Thus, you learn as an apprentice that the world is full of frightening events; you experience yourself as an impotent being, cornered by massive and inexplicable powers. Instead of fighting these forces or trying to explain them, the shaman gives up trying to change what he cannot grasp and reorients himself by adapting to their direction.

The average person, whom don Juan calls a "phantom," attempts to hold these forces at bay and refuses to sense his own impotence. The average person, your own naive unconsciousness, leads you to believe that medicine will heal your body, that psychology will make you more reasonable, and that being nice will help you in your relationship problems. Prayer should reduce the impact of fate, and technology will tame the universe. Whatever happens, you cling to the belief that you will either be saved from the unknown or discover new solutions to your problems. You believe that you are the center of a world that belongs to you.

Only your momentary terror and insecurity betray your impotence. The wiser part of you, your sorcerer, realizes that life is ultimately something beyond your mind and changing body. No one theory can completely explain anything, and the origins of even your simplest impulses seem to be connected with the universe itself. In light of this, the apprentice tries to befriend the unknown.

The shaman's apprentice takes this viewpoint and attempts to transform the onslaught of fate into an ally, as an experience of her own depths and energies, which empower her and also bring her greater mystery. During one of their early talks in *Journey to Ixtlan,* don Juan warns Castaneda that sorcery will not help him live a better life. In fact, becoming a warrior blocks you, making each step more complicated and dangerous than the last.

This warning describes the awesome nature of the path of knowledge. Anything leading to this path, whether psychology, shamanism, or meditation practice, should not advertise itself as the way to peace and harmony, for the path may also lead to the opposite. Heightened awareness invites greater discovery and opens you up to forces that press you to live, express, and accept their natures as yourself. This, in turn, brings you into conflict again and again with your own identity and your community.

Relaxation, peace, healing, and bliss are interludes in the encounter with your totality. We need a new term that encompasses the entire process of discovery and adventure, the terrifying and awesome nature of our world. While everyone is looking for healing and love, the shaman's apprentice also looks for trouble and oneness with nature.

A man I encountered during a conference in Japan had studied a smattering of Western psychology and was plagued by dreams. He literally begged me to help him with what he called his "shadow." He said the shadow had approached him in more than two hundred dreams, terrifying him and demanding unknown things. When I asked him to show me his shadow, he instantly fell into a swoon, but before I could catch him, he suddenly leapt through the air like a martial artist and began to strike. Everyone watching, including myself, was spellbound.

While we wrestled, I spoke to him and recommended that he feel even more deeply into who he was and with whom he was struggling. He responded by snorting and acting like a demon. "I want your eyes, your heart, and your mind," he screamed as his shadow, while we flew and rolled on the ground. He screeched like a disembodied spirit, in languages that were utterly foreign to me. When the furious battle broke for a moment, I encouraged the spirit to show itself more.

Suddenly the man sobbed and told me that his suffering had begun years ago when he had tried to correct his appearance by having surgery on his slightly crossed eyes. What he did not realize at the time was that an unknown and inexplicable force was behind his appearance, the thing he called his shadow, the demon he was personifying. When the force could no longer manifest itself physically through his eyes, it became furious.

The man suddenly realized that behind his disability had been an inexplicable force, a potential spirit power, an ally. He said that knowing the ally would connect him to the natural history of Japan, to Shintoism, to the freedom of Zen, to his own totality. This man was standing smack between his demon and the world of ordinary people.

So you see, opening up to knowledge makes the sorcerer more vulnerable than an average person. On the one hand, people around her fear, hate, and become jealous of her moves; on the other, the inexplicable powers that surround her become even more dangerous if she ignores them.

This man had been caught between his self-hatred and the power of the ally, his appearance and his powers. If he got too close to the ally, he would upset the world; if he remained too far away from his demon, it would kill him by making him so violent. His ally had been using his crossed eyes to express itself and therefore had become furious after the operation. This man had a truly inexplicable and powerful ancient appearance. His "shadow" was a dreamingbody that had first appeared in his eye problem.

At one time or another, we all live between two impossible worlds: the world of everyday reality and the world of inexplicable nature. Personal growth, therefore, is a process that can only be survived by a warrior, someone who battles and mediates between the ruling social powers of the world and the forces of the unknown.

But all of this is too quickly said, too far ahead of time. First you must understand that taking the path of self-knowledge means facing problems like cramps, depressions, deaths, and the misunderstandings and anger of those around you, as if all of these were your own potential power. Without stating their intentions directly, shamans teach you to prepare to survive the onslaughts of life by following and apprehending what at first appear to be unacceptable experiences.

1. Consider your personal path of development. Find the elements this path shares with shamanism, such as an initial vision or "calling," the first and second attentions, altered states of consciousness, lucid dreaming, and so on.

2. What do you call inexplicable forces on your path? Do they appear as illnesses, dreams, jealous friends, ambition? Name these forces.

3. Identify inexplicable or apparently insurmountable forces that are pulling at you now.

4. Use your imagination and consider the possibility that these inexplicable forces are potentially useful powers of your own. Imagine owning instead of disavowing them.

5. Imagine where and how you might use these forces.

6. Note how you are now living between the fear of these forces and the fear of the misunderstanding that people around you might have if you lived these forces more directly.

CHAPTER 4

FIRST
LESSONS

Your first shamanic lesson will probably be that nature is a wonderful ally that teaches you how to live. Just listen to her. It is no surprise that on one of their first walks together, don Juan says enigmatically to Castaneda that the environment is living, that plants are alive and can feel everything. At that very moment, a strong wind blows through the desert chaparral around them. Don Juan tells Castaneda that the breeze agrees with him.

Shamans treat the environment as if it were filled with knowing spirits that agree and disagree with your path. Our healers in Africa and Australia referred to the environment as the guide that would give us the timing for the next steps. On both continents, my wife, Amy, and I have had to wait hours or even days for the "right time." These people explain that experiences and ideas must be at one with the environment; they belong to the world around us.

A Taoist would say that the power of shamanism comes from the Tao. A physicist might explain that a nonlocal connection links different points in the world's field. Jung would have called this connection between the wind and the ideas of don Juan a synchronicity, that is, a coupling between two seemingly unlikely events felt by the person experiencing them to be meaningful. Shamanism reminds you that the environment has its own intelligence and is a part of you.

Native spirituality is based upon the sense that plants are alive and feel. They are our brothers and sisters. An Australian aborigine speaks in the following story about the earth's consciousness and about how one must not even play with it. He speaks of his father. "When I was 16 years old my father taught me to sing some of the songs that talk about the land. . . . One day, I went fishing with Dad. As I was walking along behind him I was dragging my spear on the beach which was leaving a long line behind me. He told me to stop doing that. He continued telling me that if I made a mark, or dig, with no reason at all, I've been hurting the bones of the traditional people of that land. We must only dig and make marks on the ground when we perform or gather food."[1]

According to aboriginal thinking, Dreamings, or ancestral entities, have created the earth's geology; these entities are alive and dreaming up events right now. I take a phenomenological approach to experiences in which we sense the environment as dreaming, as having a mind of its own. I call the sense, or communication channel for environmental experience, the "world channel."

Each of us has many different channels for perceiving and expressing information. You have visual and auditory senses through which you see and hear. You sense yourself through feeling, through movement, and through other people. You also have a world channel through which you communicate with the world in ways that cannot always be reduced to the physics of seeing and hearing. Until modern times, the Hopi Indians thought that we communicated with plants through the tops of our heads. For them, the world channel sensory apparatus was there. I consider this channel to be as important as our sensory channels.

During another walk, don Juan states that there is nothing to learn about plants because no intellectual formula can be used to understand them. At that moment, the roar of a low-flying jet startles Castaneda. Don Juan is thrilled and uses the excitement of the moment to exclaim once again that the world agrees with him.

To our native mind, our shamanic heart, the "world" means everything on earth: leaves, breezes, airplanes. Everything in your world is part of your process. In your natural mind, there are no mysterious connections or synchronicities. There is no wilderness. Everything is part of you. Neither is the world statistical. The indigenous paradigm does not split psyche from matter, inner from outer. Like the Yogi who discovers that he is, in fact, the Atman, or the whole world, the native person lives as if the world were her partner and herself.

European scientists and philosophers as early as the sixteenth century assumed that the world was separate from us; it was something outside. Alchemists, forerunners of modern science, believed that the different elements of our personalities must be "cooked" before they combined to create the *unus mundus,* or mystical "one world." In their model of transformation, discussed by Jung in his *Psychology and Alchemy,* the different elements of the world are separated. The labor of transforming these elements is called the *opus magnus,* or great work.

The alchemical recipe for incorporating the environment into your psychology went something as follows: First you unify your mental and intellectual parts to create the *unio mentalis,* a sort of mental harmony, by working out conflicts in your head. Then you join these mental solutions with the body, creating what they called the *caelum,* literally "sky" or "heaven." I think the alchemists were intuiting something like bodywork here: You must feel and express in movement what you think. After mental states combined with the body, in the final phase of the great work, the *caelum* connected with the environment. This created the *unus mundus,* in which everything coexists as one field, one world.

The *unus mundus* was a psycho-spiritual unified field concept, which is probably why Jung stated in his *Mysterium Conjuntionis* that alchemists' work would connect physics and psychology, and why it would become so important in the future of therapy. It seems to me, in looking back today on alchemical tradition and the scientific or post-Cartesian European philosophy that followed, today's problems in physics, having to do with the separation of psyche from soma, mind from matter, body from environment, came from forgetting the alchemist's *unus mundus.*

Native thinking started from an entirely different paradigm, in which nature and mind were one. For nomadic people everywhere who live closely connected to the environment, being congruent with the world is not merely a theory or a philosophy, but a matter of life and death. If you are not at one with the environment, you could sleep in the wrong place and become the prey of animals.

Indigenous peoples suffer from the insensitivity of modern, industrialized nations that destroy power spots to make superhighways, burn rainforests to make houses, and put state parks and recreation areas on ancient burial grounds. This destructive style of relating to the world is manifest not only in air and water pollution, but in how you repress your own nature by failing to develop the second attention that experiences the earth as mysterious and alive.

For me, indigenous thinking is the basis of group process. The group expresses itself through individuals and the environment, and vice versa. In a way, there is no individual or group work; everything you do is processing the events of nature. To reincorporate or discover the environment's spirit in everyday life is to view people and their surroundings as one being. If, for example, I ask one member of a couple, family, or group a question, it can be a perceptual prejudice to expect an answer from the individual addressed. The answer may come from any part of the environment; someone else may speak up, or the environment may announce itself in other ways. Of course, there are times when each person must speak for himself, but you should be careful not to become one-sidedly attached to the paradigm that the individual is located only in your own body. You must consider the possibility that each of us is a channel for the world, just as the world is a channel for each of us.

There are times when you are alone in nature and feel united with the environment. You feel the world around you as if it were a body part or a partner, sending you messages of agreements and disagreements, pleasure and stress. This sense is crucial if you need to fish or hunt to eat. But the way that native people relate to the environment is more than a matter of survival. It is the basis of their spiritual traditions and an integral part of their psychology. Sensing this voice of the natural environment can be an important method of self-protection and a path to knowledge.

I remember giving a workshop with native North American shamans, friends of mine from the Canadian Pacific Northwest. I often begin my seminars by meeting people, but as our seminar commenced near a river in central Oregon, these people did a fire ritual for the spirits in the environment. As these spirits were unable to arrive the first day, on the second evening they offered plates of food and glasses of beer to the spirits and communed with them. After the fire had burned down, they explained that the spirits must have been a Native American and a white person who had died recently. Their information matched the details of a description of two people we heard about later who had recently died in that area. The shamans said that the reason some of the seminar participants had slept restlessly the first night was that the fire ritual for the spirits in the environment had not been done. Sure enough, after the burning, the spirits let everyone rest better than they had the first night.

Personal History

When the world speaks to you, it is impossible to tell whether the world is doing things to you or you are doing things to it. You may perceive yourself as causing some events and being the recipient of others, but you never know for sure whether you send messages and get responses or whether the world sends you messages to which you respond.

This inherent message symmetry or invariance means that you cannot assume that you are the center of the universe, initiating or creating things. You are an aspect of the world. This radical shift in identity from being the center to being a participant is the goal of mystical and spiritual traditions.

Sensing yourself as a part of the entire world would create an identity crisis if you let yourself experience the environment. However, synchronicities, though momentarily shocking, are not enough to shake apprentices like you and me out of our person-centered world. We may need another lesson.

Buddhist teachings, shamanistic rituals, and simply the process of aging imply that your personal identity will soon disappear. Personal history is your identity, the role you have in a given community and world. You are the man, woman, mother, father, wife, husband, partner, student, mechanic, teacher; the Protestant, Catholic, Jew, Mohammedan, Buddhist; the African, American, European, Australian, Japanese, Indian; and so on. You are all of these things and more. You identify with your past and present pursuits, your gifts and your problems.

You must erase your personal history; otherwise, you are at the mercy of what others think. Your identity limits you by forcing you into a social role or mold needed by your community. In this sense, other people's thoughts of you have power over you. If you are a Native American and begin to study at the university, your brothers and sisters might be suspicious of your new endeavor. If you are a homemaker and begin to study, your household may resent you. If you are a minister and talk about God as the environment, you may run into trouble with the modern church. If you are a woman and decide not to marry, your family may reject you. If you are gay or lesbian, the world may disown you. Your world projects its gifts and problems upon your identity and in this way takes away your personal freedom to be who you are. Nevertheless, you detach from your personal history, consciously or unconsciously, in many ways. Altered states of consciousness, such as fury and ecstasy, may disturb your identity. When you fall in love with a forbidden person, you find yourself in conflict with who you were. Your personal history is shaken when you study forbidden subjects, are near death, or become ill; when a partner dies or leaves; or when your children grow up.

Either you detach yourself from your personal history or you begin to fear that death or injury will remove it for you. Life consists of continually facing the terror and pleasure of becoming a new individual without history. I know from my study of childhood dreams that removing personal history is the crucial lesson that everyone seems destined to learn from birth. Your earliest memories or dreams often involve a dramatic conflict and threat to your identified self; demons, witches, and monsters chase you.

If powerful allies appear as antagonists in your earliest dreams, your myth is to confront an ally, whether you agree to this encounter or not. As you live, you confront your mythical attackers in many forms until you change the way in which you define yourself. During certain periods of your life, the attack seems to abate, yet it returns again to provoke you to remove personal history.

It is as if you live and die many times. It seems sometimes as if you have just one central lesson to learn: to continuously drop all sorts of rigid identities. The Taoists and

Buddhists put it briefly: Everything is impermanent. Instead of realizing this, however, you find yourself looking forward to some ideal time when you shall achieve freedom from the battle between yourself and your dreams, believing that if you could overcome your problems you would be free. You find yourself attracted to stories in which the hero's life hangs upon the outcome of a dramatic battle between himself and a challenger from the beyond.

You make decisions to try to change in one direction or to adopt a program that changes you, substituting one identity for another or blending the two. You even try to give up your old self and identify with something new and useful. But your life may still be a mess, as you are troubled by chronic ailments and relationship conflicts.

Finally the point arrives when the more you change, the more you sense the complexity of it all. Changing identities, even becoming free from a previous inhibition, is not enough. The process of creating and dropping personal history leads to the discovery that you are neither this nor that, but the awareness of it all.

Shamanic dismemberment or initiation rituals mirror this peak experience.[2] In these, the apprentice or seeker meets incredible forces—vicious demons—and undergoes unthinkable torture while her body is torn apart and dismembered in visions. The symbolism of having the limbs and intestines taken out and later replaced reflects the experiences many people go through over a period of ten or even twenty years. Chronic illness, feelings of being torn asunder by opposing forces, and near-death experiences frequently have the goal of "cleansing" you from your own self and refilling you with nothingness or with pure nature. During such difficult times, you are forced to undo yourself, to go to pieces, to free yourself from the tendency to think of yourself at any given time as one type of person with one type of task. Either you become fluid, or nature erases you in its own way.

This reminds me of one of my clients who was sitting in meditation, working on an inner dialogue. Visions and body sensations arose as part of her mental flux. Suddenly, out of nowhere, a voice came to her and said that she would lose the baby she was then carrying. The voice sent her into a great shock, compounded by the fact that she had waited until her late thirties to become pregnant and was now in her eighth month.

Tearfully, she told me that having a baby had become her greatest wish. The baby would fulfill and finally satisfy the expectations of her relatives. What could I say? "Find out who stands behind that voice," I suggested.

She turned inside and told me that the voice belonged to God. "He said I should either give up my identity as a mother and become a student or he would kill me," she reported. She decided immediately to take up her new studies. A few weeks later, her baby was born as healthy as could be, but because of an unusual accident in the hospital the child was killed before it was three days old. My client was as prepared as she could be for this tragedy. She dropped her personal history as a mother as fluidly as she could and lived on according to the new direction of her fate. God may have erased her baby, but she had erased herself first.

Uprooting personal history usually involves a great deal of pain. Years of unbearable suffering generally precede the transformation presaged by death. You spend a lot of time struggling against fate. Fate always seems so precarious, always threatening you with symptoms and difficulties beyond your ability to solve.

One of the most remarkable things about the African healers whom Amy and I visited was that they were detached from their own personal history. Even though we are white, they blessed us as Africans after taking us through a ritual of exchanging our clothes for the cloth of the equatorial bush. We found that it was just this respect for their tradition and detachment from it that was so healing.

Don Juan, too, unlike many Native American seers today, was detached from his own history, even from his own community. We know from Castaneda's later books that don Juan almost died several times. He was even buried once, prematurely. As he grew older, he consciously removed his personal history, broke with his past, and opened his heart to the world around him. He grew beyond the one-sidedness of identifying solely as a Native American who hated European-American invaders. He loved his heritage but culled its essence and grew beyond it by letting go of his hatred for his enemies. He realized that his parents had died tragically because they could not let go of their desire for revenge against their Mexican persecutors. He said that they lived and died like American Indians, without realizing above all that life is too short to have just one identity.

Death as an Adviser

There are times when you want to die, and all of us will die one day. Separating from an old identity, system, or relationship is like dying. I realize only after one of these separations that I have died. Since I am so stubborn, it takes a lot to kill me, and I die painfully and unconsciously. Afterward I reflect and realize what has happened, like the spirit of a dead man who leaves his body and only then awakens to what has happened to him.

There are easier methods. If you give them a chance, fantasies of death will erase your personal history: the way in which you work, the expectations you have of yourself, and your predictable and worn-out patterns of relating to others. According to a Buddhist ritual, you must meditate on your death every day. Many teachers agree that death is the only wise adviser you have.

Were it not for fear of death, you might never have the courage to change and jump over the obstacles created by history. When you use death as an adviser, however, you remember that you can no longer put off detaching from yourself and your apparent significance or insignificance.

Think of a client of mine who recently died. When she had come to see me for the first time, she was dying of cancer, and her tumors were beginning to inhibit her breathing. She wanted to see me because she was terrified of death. I asked her if there were still something she would like to do with her life and urged her to follow her most important wish. She said immediately that she wanted to fulfill a lifelong dream and travel to Finland in the summer.

"Go ahead," I said. "Take a trip to Finland."

"Oh no," she answered, "I couldn't do that. My husband hasn't any free time just now. He has to work."

That conversation took place in May. Instead of taking time off from work and going to Finland, her husband took time off in July, just when his vacation time came up, to bury and mourn his wife. Death meant little to that woman. Everything else took precedence: her husband's job, her children, her household. She spent her life postponing the things that meant the most to her so that she could maintain her personal history as a housewife. She could have used her death as a wise ally if she had been prepared to experience her disease as a force asking her to free herself from her personal identity. Instead, it simply erased her.

Such near-death situations can make death, in the form of terrifying diseases or body experiences, appear as your wise dreamingbody adviser, the best and most trustworthy one you have. From this viewpoint, fearing death or even getting ill is a fortunate experience because it signifies detachment from your identity.

Every time you fear the worst or are preparing to defend yourself against inner or outer forces, experiment first with imagining your own demise. Feel what it might be like to die. Even go through the act of dying. Imagine how you will die, what you will look like, what you will experience. It is important not only to think that you are going to die, but to imagine what will happen next.

Go through the details of the death fantasy, whether it is of falling off a cliff, dying of cancer, or being struck by an automobile. These fantasies are trying to get you unstuck. Bury yourself. Die before you die. Write your own epitaph: Here lies poor, little old me. He did some things well but could not make the turn and allow the new me to happen. He died at that point so that now I can live on, free. Now I am not myself anymore but have been replaced by taking part in and witnessing whatever is happening.

Taking Responsibility

Responsibility is an important word in psychology, for it connects you to everything you experience. The following story about don Juan sounds like it came straight from modern therapy. During their first meeting, Castaneda lied to don Juan, bragging about his knowledge of plants in order to impress the old Indian with his intelligence. Don Juan immediately recognized the lie. What bothered him, though, was not the lie itself but Castaneda's attitude toward it. Castaneda had not taken his own story seriously. He had not taken responsibility for it; he did not believe his own lie.

Taking responsibility means accepting everything you say, feel, hear, write, see, and communicate as part of you. Accepting your accidents and your lies is an act of compassion. Taking responsibility means that if you are sick, you must understand that the body is bringing up a dream you have not yet known. If you have relationship difficulties, accidents, or world problems, things are happening to you with which you are not in agreement. Taking responsibility means focusing awareness not only upon the events you identify with but also upon the events you want to disavow.

Taking responsibility requires appreciating what happens to you as potentially valuable. Such an attitude belongs to shamans, therapists, and Taoists. It also appears in Zen. The Zen master in Kyoto said, "Every day is a fine day," meaning that whatever happens is just perfect: Use it, pick it up, and find its meaning.

But taking responsibility requires more than having the right attitude. You need to pick up your secondary process. I remember bragging to Amy some time ago about my relationship to a well-known political figure. I said, "Oh, yes, I worked with so-and-so and his whole family years ago." I knew that the therapeutic ethic required confidentiality. I was not supposed to talk about my clients to anyone, not even my wife. Not only had I broken a professional code, but I had done it in a boastful tone: "See me. Notice how important I am," I had said.

I caught myself, however, and decided to use my second attention. I was disgusted by myself. I could hardly believe that I would brag. After all, I already had as much public support as I needed. Why had I done such a stupid thing? Why had I needed to be seen? Instead of answering these questions, I tried to take responsibility for my act as if it had come from a part of me that was trying to be heard.

Finally, I dove into the experience, consciously bragged, and discovered that I wanted to be taken even more seriously than I had been. At that point in time, I was afraid to bring my ideas forward in public about controversial issues; I was a political wimp. I preferred to identify myself as a psychologist and was shy about being a social activist. The discovery of my inner, disavowed need to be heard was the beginning of much of my public work and of my writing the book *The Leader as Martial Artist*.

If you catch yourself bragging unconsciously, brag consciously. If you are like some people who say that they do not lie, then I want to advise that you try to make up a lie. Practice lying about yourself. If you take responsibility for doing that, your lie can be unfolded as being part of your task, even a part of your personal myth.

All other concepts of shamanism may be found within the idea of taking responsibility. As you take responsibility for the world around us, you find synchronicity or agreements. You find the erasure of personal history, because bragging and lying are not part of your normal identity. Your lies are the stories not of your personal identity, but of someone you are not yet identifying with. Taking responsibility includes using death as an adviser. In a world where life is so short, you cannot afford to neglect anything you do. Each act is one of potential significance.

1. Be aware of the environment. Imagine that the natural world around you is alive and can speak to you. Listen, smell, feel, and look at the signals that the environment emits. Hold such perceptions with your second attention and follow them. What is the environment saying to you? Don't be afraid of projecting.

2. Experiment with telling a lie. Tell a lie to yourself, in your imagination. Try lying even if you are shy or embarrassed about doing so. Tell the lie as if you were a great story-teller. This may be difficult, because mythmaking is a deep process, but try until a real lie turns into a story with a beginning and an end.

Take a few minutes to do this.

Telling a lie can be embarrassing, because you expose your deepest dreams and fantasies of becoming a ruler or a magician, of having more sexual prowess and beauty than others, of having more money, more friends, or more power. But remember, you are not just telling a lie. You are creating a myth. Consider your lie to be true. How are you already living this myth? Take a few minutes to experiment. Act like the person in your lie. Consider changing your personal identity if necessary in order to live closer to your myth. How have your dreams already discussed this change?

3. Drop your personal history and use death as an adviser. To begin, describe yourself: Who are you normally? What have you been doing? From what kind of family do you come? Describe your gender, race, religion, profession, and nationality. How do you see your body? Is it weak or strong, ugly or beautiful? Are you successful, or not?

Go into a fantasy you have had about your death. Describe how you imagine death coming to you.

Experiment with letting this fantasy of death take over. Let go of your ordinary identity you described in the beginning of this exercise. Imagine why death might want this identity to die. What part of you is meant to die, so to speak?

Imagine and enjoy, if possible, the detachment that comes from death.

Imagine and experience living the freedom of your death in life, in the moment, at work, in relationships, and in the world.

CHAPTER 5

THE HUNTER

There is no single shamanic calling that is enough. The spirit must be consulted and agree at every stage of a shamanic apprenticeship. In Africa our healers had to go into trance just to ask if they could continue with our healing ceremony. In Australia we had to wait for the right "time."

Before I begin professional training with someone, I wait for a convincing dream of my own or from my client. Sometimes I consult the *I Ching*. Without such oracles or dreams, there is no certainty that our training will be of use to the client or that she has chosen the right profession.

Before Castaneda was ready to progress in his apprenticeship, don Juan had to determine whether Carlos had the agreement of the earth to continue on the Yaqui Way of Knowledge. So don Juan proposed an entrance test into the training. Castaneda had to use his body to find a "place of power" in the desert chaparral.

The Spot

Compared to state licensing tests and the graduate exams of our institutes and universities, shamanic testing strikes us as being absurd. It requires good omens. You cannot prepare for it intellectually. Today's licensing procedures to practice medicine and psychology are based upon the belief that a practitioner must be able to regurgitate accepted knowledge under stress. But shamanic testing is based upon another reality. This testing procedure requires that you be able to follow your body instincts to survive on this earth. It requires connection to nature. If you pick the wrong place to camp for the night, it could be your last sleep.

The spot you find must be your friend, a place where you feel well and rested. Remember that the shaman, by definition, differs from his tribal family in his ability to heal himself. Since illness or disease is a signal from your dreamingbody for you to recognize its existence, the shaman can be redefined as someone who has more ability than others to follow the sensations of his dreamingbody. If you follow your body's sensations and dreams, you are automatically on the right spot; you feel physically alive, simultaneously stimulated and peaceful.

Thus, it makes sense for a shaman to choose her apprentices based on their ability to heal themselves by finding the right spot. Many shamanic apprentices suffer terrible fates: They are severely overweight, crazy, deformed, or half-mad. Some behave like ordinary people. But all seem to find the right teacher and attain the healing they need.

Shamanic initiations tend to make it seem that the spirits' power alone must rescue the apprentices from the hands of death. But this opinion does not give the apprentices enough credit, for if they are apprentices, they are almost by definition able to follow the powers of the dreamingbody within themselves. At another point in time, when the apprentice becomes a healer or teacher himself, he helps others not only by his powers, but by his ability to help them find their own dreamingbodies. This may be why many healers say it is not the healer who heals, but the ability of the spirit and the client's or apprentice's own ability to find "the right spot" of healing or knowledge.

Early on in my studies, I experimented with the problem of finding the right spot and went off with other learners on a meditation retreat. We decided to work together in a small garden next to the house in which we were staying. We posed ourselves the task of finding our own "spots," our places of well-being in the garden. But the first spot I wanted to sit down on had already been taken by someone else.

Finally, after I had walked around for some time, my body took me to a most unlikely place, a steep incline at the edge of the garden. There I lay on my back, upside down, my head facing downhill, my feet in the air. I was surprised that my body felt so good in such an awkward position.

I discovered that finding the right spot depends not only on body sense, but also upon what is happening in the world around you at a given moment. Any spot you choose is connected to the entire field of the natural environment, people, and spirits. The spot you are required to find represents the role you are asked to play in the field at a given moment, and the role you play is the one that is best for everyone and everything around you at that moment. The moment I lay on my back with my head downhill, I was not needed in other spots. My job at that moment, so to speak, was to be upside down and backward.

Finding the right spot on earth is a matter of world channel awareness. The shaman identifies her spot as one of healing and self-protection. As long as you live in this field, you are always being tested, without realizing it. You must constantly ask yourself, Where am I living? Can I find my spot in this field? Is my present spot the right spot? Is it a proper picture of who I am and what is trying to happen to me?

When you move about in the everyday world, are you aware of the power of certain places? Be careful about where you sit at work, where you sit when you eat. Can you sense which spirits are good for you and which are bad? Is that dirty street corner, the beach by the sea, or a hilly spot in a long-forgotten garden the right spot? It is finally your ability to follow your dreamingbody that gives you a sense of security and well-being.

In searching for a spot, remember that the place your body chooses is not always the place your mind wants. Your true spot is an aspect of fate. It is the bioregion you are meant to be living in. It is a fate that has opened up to you because the universe needs you to play this role for its own momentary wholeness.

The Tools of the Hunter

The spirit determines when and how training can continue. Don Juan interprets Castaneda's falling asleep on a restful spot as a sign of success. His apprenticeship may continue, but Castaneda's involvement now takes on serious dimensions. He can no longer just dabble in his apprenticeship. His apparently academic interest in psychotropic plants transforms into a fascination with don Juan's way of knowledge.

Dabbling in shamanism, psychology, or meditation often hides a fascination with altered states of consciousness that come to you as if they wanted you to go more deeply into them. It may even seem to you as if your interest were a matter of life and death. You might say that the process has chosen you in spite of yourself. At first, shamanism tempts you through the media of your interests and studies; then it challenges you through a teacher; and suddenly it threatens to become a life-and-death issue or a lifelong project.

You find yourself in the midst of a fascinating and unconquerable area where you are no longer in control. You seem to be navigating in psychic territory, and your past interests and background are unable to help you meet the terrifying spirits at the perimeter of consciousness. Illness, relationship problems, addictions, or social conflict rob you of your freedom. You seem to need new tools to live through these experiences. Regardless of where the initiation into human mysteries takes place, it always feels like more than you can handle. Even though you are right here with everyone and everything else, it is as if you were walking upon another planet, and you are afraid even to trust your own body. You have only your meager psychic tools and courage to help.

Shamans who refer to their work as hunting are hunting power. Many South American healers refer to their work of searching for healing and psychotropic plants as hunting. Hunters will always hunt, probably because of the basic need I believe we all have to be whole and to alter our states of consciousness through one method or another.

Hunting for mind-altering substances and changes in consciousness is in your nature; it is a sort of talent. A talent, a professional ability, or a gift operates independently of intent, once it is learned. Your talents even imprison you by happening compulsively. A true calling is like an addiction that must be nourished. A great musician, for example, not only is talented but is possessed by her musical demon. If you deny a talent's existence, it will suck the energy it requires, and you may feel depressed without knowing why. In my opinion, it is the unconscious interest and talent in hunting power that has addicted many indigenous people to drugs like alcohol.

A related talent connected to an interest in shamanism is the art of living. It appears autonomously at first, in your mystical, therapeutic, and shamanic interests, your spiritual aspirations, and your fascination with altered states of consciousness. It makes you think that everything you learn about the dreaming world is more than a teaching: It is a way of life. This is why even students of psychology, the most rational aspect of shamanism, may make spiritual sects out of what they are learning. The many hundreds of such people we have met in different countries seem to want more than healing and insight. They are searching for a way of life. They need to live ecstatically, and nothing short of this makes them happy.

The hunt for power and ecstasy behaves like an autonomous and creative drive, appearing in dreams, spirits in the night, personal problems, or the fear of death, propelling you to live fully and to find meaning in everything. Therapy, healing, and teaching are only some, perhaps even limiting, contexts for this talent. Becoming a hunter and a warrior, a shaman, is a wider context. Doing so means nothing less than learning to live life by improvising from one moment to the next. Teachers of shamanism, psychology, meditation, and the future of personal transformation must address this context.

As a hunter, you must study the rational details of energy, of "psychic prey." You are doing more than just learning about the signals of the unknown. You are developing the ability to notice and to follow signs that give greater access to life, to the energy that makes every moment exciting and awesome. You are waiting to gain the courage to drop your ordinary way of living.

The Hunter and the Hunted

First lessons of shamanism, psychology, meditation, or even social work sound like behavioral or moral prescriptions: "Do this, then that." Don Juan explains the steps in the hunter's training, beginning with the relationship to nature. In his review of what happened when he killed a snake, don Juan explains that he had to apologize to the animal for cutting off its life so abruptly. He did this realizing that his life, too, would one day be cut off in a similar fashion; thus, the prey and its hunter were one.

The insight that you are not only the killer, but one who someday will also be wiped out, gives you compassion for everything. You are the persecutor and the victim and, even more, the observer and the facilitator of your process. You are the one who has dreams and who is the dreammaker, who suffers from symptoms and the creative power behind your symptoms. Best of all, you are, or could be, the facilitator between both the symptoms and the power.

In other words, as a hunter, you know that you are simultaneously various parts of the world and the facilitator of those parts. You are the doer and the one done to, the seer and the seen. You are the one struggling under the pain of life, the one who creates the pain, and the one who must facilitate between the two. You are the student and also the teacher of perennial philosophies. Each time you learn something or have an enriching experience, you honor the universe from which this came by thanking it. You are the student and the universe.

Everything is connected, and nothing happens without warning, though you may experience it as such. Don Juan says that a hunter is "tight"; he or she knows that everything is connected and therefore leaves little to chance.[1] As a hunter, you not only experience life but take responsibility for helping to create it by being "tight" and noticing the normal as well as the accidental.

The ordinary hunter's prey includes the plants and animals of the earth: nourishing herbs, snakes, deer—the living beings that give you life. But for a shaman's apprentice, prey is not only the flesh of living plants and animals. It is the sense of mystery that gives you a special presence and love for life.

As a hunter, you know that certain signals are your prey; they are special signs of nature. These are things like perceptual irregularities, such as flickering thoughts and visual or auditory hallucinations. The shaman may call her prey the spirits or ghosts or spooks that inspire, heal, and destroy—familiars that guide her and drive her crazy. Just as therapists prey on different forms of consciousness, energy, and process, the warrior hunts power objects and situations that are unusual.

In some Eastern traditions, the prey might be called the Chi, or Ki, energy. In other parts of the world, particularly

Haiti, it is voodoo. Some therapists hunt dreams or dream figures; the body-oriented processworker would call her prey the dreamingbody. Meditation procedures call prey the feelings and thoughts that pass through us. Psychological schools focus upon moods, dreams, and complexes. All these are processes, double signals, and the living unconscious. I call all prey the Tao. Some refer to this as good or bad luck.

Whatever name the mystery goes by, it is the source of power, of healing, of liveliness, and of fun. What do you call the signs of this mysterious something that revives and cares for you? What do you call your guides? What are their routines? How tight, or perceptive, are you at finding these signs? If your hunting ability is keen and sharp, your prey is seconds away from your awareness in any situation, at any time of day or night.

Since sensing prey is an unusual or accidental process, we might call it a secondary process, an unexpected, incomplete message that appears through one or more of your sensory channels of awareness. Sometimes you experience the prey in a vague sensation and unusual feeling, intuition, or thought. You feel but cannot explain it. The routines of your prey are inexplicable, confusing, or chaotic signals received in various channels of communication: seeing, hearing, sensing, feeling, moving, and interacting with people and outer events.

Practice seeing hallucinations. Hear voices that are not there. Feel body experiences that you cannot explain, and notice weird movements in yourself. Watch for paranoid fantasies about others. Catch and follow them. Some doctors will warn you that you are listening to absurdities and that you should not dabble in nonrealities. But if you have the calling of a shaman, you must listen to and catch the prey before it takes your energy.

Experience yourself at your worst and your best, as others do, in your imagination, and try to love or hate yourself as others do. Don't just take your fantasies as signs of high or low self-esteem. Experience the power behind them, behind love and recriminations, and use this power constructively. Notice spontaneous events that are in agreement or disagreement with you, and catch them, eat them. The unpredictable visual, auditory, proprioceptive, kinesthetic, relationship, and world channel events are your nourishment. Don't just listen to New Age or mainstream talk about your perceptions. Experience them for yourself. Catch them and ride them like waves on a sea.

Some of the routines of your prey are not chaotic but predictable. For example, the content of your fantasies can be predicted from your dreams. The shamanic hunter masters awareness by using his second attention to notice inner feelings and fantasies and unusual outer signals from the environment. He feels things and senses the unknown parts of himself, even before they force themselves upon him. He follows and supports the irrational and uncanny, that which belongs to the nagual, i.e., the unconscious. He knows that his power lies in catching and tracing his double signals, his own incongruities, dreams, fantasies, and symptoms.

In relationships, he notices his own double signals: the inexplicable sound of his voice, the movements of his hands—all of those signals that do not go along with what he is saying. And he notices incongruities in those around him. This is the prey he is hunting and the power he needs to carry him closer to his potential.

As a hunter in the world, you sense the atmosphere, the ambience around your family, tribe, community, business, or group. You listen to what others say, but you also sense the unspoken, emotional background, the excitement, love, jealousy, and ambition that can transport the group out of its own ordinary reality.

Being tight and knowing the routines of the prey means tracking your own behavior. In time and with training, you become aware of your own power to dance, sing, speak, feel, and communicate with the world. Consider the story of a young man I worked with in the Colorado mountains. He was meditating on the direction his life should take, hunting the future.

As we worked, he noticed something moving about outside the window. When he glanced outside, he thought, for a split second, that he saw a little green man pointing in a specific direction. Being a tight hunter, the young man did not let this fantasy escape but fixed it in his vision. We got up together and followed the direction in which the green man had pointed, to a small, nearby cliff. In his fantasy, the young man heard the voice of the green man shriek, "Jump!" Feeling threatened, he sat down at the edge of the cliff with me and listened closely to the voice. "Who are you?" he asked.

He got no answer, so he kept his attention on the memory of the voice, trying to recall its tone, tempo, and nature. After a few moments, the voice returned, louder than before. "Jump!" it insisted. "Jump, or I'll push you!" Suddenly the young man noticed that his process had switched from hearing to visualizing. He now saw himself flying over the cliff and landing. But where did he land? In the general ward of a hospital in a Swiss city, not as a patient but as a doctor.

This was the answer to his question. He knew what he had to do next, and he did it. A year later, he entered the university to begin his training as a doctor. Today he works in a Swiss hospital. He told me at the time of his vision quest that he had been blocked from entering the medical profession because his father had been a doctor and he had wanted to be different.

The man had to hunt before he could become a doctor; he needed shamanic discipline more than he needed knowledge. In fact, previous knowledge may be a hindrance to learning to track the energy and process of nature. The hunter has an exacting attitude toward his process.

What is the difference between a madman and a hunter? Actually, there is little difference, which is probably why earlier researchers in shamanism thought that the shamans were psychotic or epileptic. The difference between a shaman and an ordinary person swamped by experiences is that the shaman's tightness allows her to lead an ordinary life. She knows that now she is "hunting," and now she is just shopping.

And she can differentiate herself from her prey. As a hunter, you know you are the witness and do not become entangled in your visions. You can be in and out of them at the same time, whereas someone in an "ordinary" state of consciousness is either possessed by such experiences or divorced from them. I want to stress that the way of the hunter is the way of a person who willfully chooses when to hunt and when to temporarily set powers aside. You know when to identify with and when to disidentify with your prey so that you are not its victim, not overwhelmed by experience.

But you need a special feeling to catch unusual events. You need a sense of freedom. You may finally catch your amazing prey not because of your knowledge of yourself or the environment, but because of who you are. You can only catch yourself or what you will become. In the end, you encounter and learn from incredible events because you yourself are slowly becoming incredible.

Personal History

In other words, either you are a hunter, or you become the prey. Since animals and plants have specific routines, you must be careful not to become predictable yourself. Personal history may be your own greatest danger. Personal history makes you a routine individual, the prey or victim of life. If you are not careful, even learning to hunt can make you predictable and heavy with all that you have learned. You might think, "Now I am a shaman, a psychologist, a meditator, a spiritual person, or someone who is going to help others or the world," but these labels are only the identity and may become overly predictable and rigid.

I too lose my freedom. When I was beginning this book, I kept thinking, "Now I am writing a book!" In such moments, my inadvertent self-importance created more seriousness than I needed. It was as if I were overeating. Suddenly I felt heavy, like a duck sitting in front of a hunter's gun. I was the prey I was stalking, not the hunter I wanted to be.

I can now laugh about this heavy state of affairs, but being in it was no fun. The danger of becoming like the states you are studying was called in analytic circles in the beginning of the twentieth century "falling into the unconscious," becoming depressed, inflated, or crazy. Prey for these analytic versions of ancient shamans was an image from the so-called unconscious: the gods and goddesses, the devil, the fool, and so on. My teachers implied that one had to lead a tight life, study, become knowledgeable, and fear the unknown, lest you become inundated or identified with it, becoming a Christ or a devil.

But the danger for the early students of the unconscious may have been in the very paradigm that they used: the belief that you could use the unknown or the unconscious as if it were an infinite resource that did not need anything in return. Psychology certainly has shamanistic roots, but it has somehow forgotten the ritual of honoring its resource. Psychology, without respect for the unknown, looks just like modern technology, which takes from the environment without giving back to it. It may be dangerous to delve into the unconscious for one's personal edification, to use dreams as if they were one's own.

Without an ancient and indigenous respect for the environment and its power, you identify with it and think you must be wise instead of following its wisdom. Hence, the greatest danger for helpers of all ilk is becoming possessed by the unknown and acting wise or powerful. There are too many therapists and shamans who act as if they are better than others.

This self-inflation is similar to the way in which you use the natural environment, picking out what you need instead of respecting it as the source of life. Without your respect for its awesome nature, without thanks, the environment seems to rebel and threaten you. Everyone touching any aspect of shamanism faces the danger of self-importance: Nature rebels by terrifying you and by gobbling up your humanness, leaving you as nothing more than an inflated blimp, fearing your death.

As a tight hunter, you are wary and retain the possibility of not being like the prey you are after. Zen refers to this fluid and free state of mind as beginner's mind. The beginner is humble, open, and aware of what is happening, experiencing life without preconceived judgments. A beginner's mind is not the same as an empty mind, though. Keido Fukushima of Kyoto, a Zen master, understands this state of mind as being the creative mind: free, fluid, and unpredictable. The warrior is not full of routines, nor is he empty, except perhaps of his own personal history. He is free in the sense of being open to whatever is happening.

You know that you are free from routines and the importance of your personal identity and history when you laugh. Laughter can be a mixture of humor, craziness, and wisdom. In any case, when you are able to laugh, not only are you looking for life, but you are living it. With this sense of freedom, you can track certain processes that have no routines. They are the magic that makes life worth living. Unexpected events are the shaman's key to life, the mystical, incredible animals that break their own routines and that may even stop in the midst of their flight from an indigenous person so he can shoot them.[2]

Indigenous peoples say that you must apologize for killing plants and animals and also be open to whether the universe will "give" you this prey or not. Not everything is up to you. What you discover is what you are given. To find the most magical element in life and the impulse for creativity, you need to be in a special, magical mood, the mood in which you are thankful for whatever happens, even if this is nothing. In other words, the way you hunt is by being the very object of your hunting.

The opposite of the spirit is often your self-identity. By recommending that you develop a strong ego or by continually focusing upon the same problems, using the same methods, Western therapies may inadvertently solidify that very sense of personal history that could finally hinder you from finding the shaman's keys. If you always focus on the same issues, using the same methods, life begins to be predictable: You can guess your future lifestyle, the type of demons that will chase you, and the nature of the unknown that will pester you.

Regardless of how strong your routines, however, you will never be able to predict exactly when events will happen. You can guess *what* will happen, but not *when*. The ancient Chinese book of divination and wisdom, the *I Ching,* says that the spirit is mysterious, more than its manifestation in terms of the ten thousand things we see in the world. According to the *Tao Te Ching,* there are two Taos, one that can be seen and spoken about and one that can only be experienced. The crucial energy of life that you are after can be experienced in terms of the feeling you have surrounding events; it is the dynamic of a moment, not its description; the "when," not only the "what."

For example, if you had known that young man who became a doctor, you could have guessed that he would go into medicine. But who would have known exactly when that information would get to him? No one could have predicted that his vision quest would have such dramatic energy, that he would have to jump off the cliff and go over all his edges to become himself.

The timing and intensity of messages is beyond the study of routines, channels, and symptoms. The spirit behind change seems to come from nowhere and, at first inspection, seems to be nothing. Yet the greatest discovery a hunter may be able to make may be timing itself.

EXERCISES

1. Find the spot. Take a few minutes and focus on feeling your body. Scan your body with your feelings. What is happening, and where? Imagine a spot that your body needs right now to make itself feel well and healthy. If you feel well,

imagine a spot that would make you feel even better. Place yourself on that spot, in reality or in your imagination, and feel any changes that may happen. In what part of your body do they occur? Have you had any symptoms there? Does this "wellness spot" remind you of any of your dreams?

Now that you have found a good spot, ask yourself what attracted you to the areas of discomfort you were previously in.

2. If you are in the mood to practice hunting, experiment with the following. Describe and then drop your personal history—the way in which you identify yourself—for a moment, and experiment with the sense of freedom. Meditate and close your eyes, counting your breaths from one to ten each time you exhale.

Remain as aware as possible—hunt!—and notice what, if anything, disturbs your attention while you are counting breaths. Catch that thing. Focus on it. This is your prey.

Keep your focus on the experience, and study it in great detail. Track it, so to speak. Be exact in your observation. What does it do? How does it look, sound, feel, move, or relate?

Allow the disturbing experience to unfold in all of your sensory channels. Try to feel it. See it by making pictures out of it. Hear it by listening to the sounds or words it might make. Move as it would move, while still feeling, seeing, and hearing it, until you know its nature and its message. This is good hunting.

Try to use this message now.

CHAPTER 6

THE WARRIOR

The dreamingbody can be a prison. It possesses you if you don't use it consciously. Like the Yogi driven mad by the goddess Shakti, who has aroused the Kundalini in the body, the individual touched by the hunting spirit is propelled relentlessly upon the path of self-knowledge. Behind even a mild interest in shamanism can be the seeker of ecstasy.

You can never train enough in the shamanic work of hunting for lost energies and souls. Becoming any kind of facilitator for human growth, for that matter, is a task without end. Only your own dreams can measure your success at this work. Perhaps that is why shamanistic traditions around the world prescribe that success in apprenticeship be judged only by dreams, illnesses, ecstatic experiences, and master shamans.[1]

You cannot learn the skills you need through effort alone, and each situation you meet within yourself seems more impossible than the last. That is why the perennial philosophies have recommended that the best choice for the seeker of wisdom is humility. Like the holy mountain in Japan, Mount Fujiyama, which is flat and humble at the top rather than peaked and proud, the student is to rise above everyday life while being open to messages from above. At any height or degree of accomplishment, you are always a beginner.

Training

The skills of psychotherapy can be learned quickly, yet it takes many years of practical work before you believe in yourself. During training, you continually doubt your abilities at your chosen profession. One reason for this is that, though you want to be sufficiently prepared to deal with fate, you never can be. The job is just too complex and full of inexplicable forces. It is an inflation to think that you can manage the spirit. At best, you can learn to follow it.

So your doubts can be useful; they force you to learn about things you do not know about. It takes weeks to learn skills but much longer to acquire those special attitudes that shamans passed down through personal instruction to their apprentices. What makes the shaman's apprentice in any kind of soul work most insecure is the sense of insufficient contact with the spirit. Only continuous contact with the unknown gives you the right feeling for the work; you are a student of change, not the changer.

As the number of people interested in personal and organizational growth increases, psychotherapy and its associated professions will become mainstream. As a result, the number of public regulations and requirements for facilitators, healers, therapists, and doctors is growing. The public tries to ensure the quality of its mental health and community workers by creating regulations based upon purely rational considerations.

To function in helpful or healing capacities, you need to have experience in areas of human concern, matters of life and death, psychosis, extreme states, medicine, and politics. But your personal development is crucial as well. And it is just this development that public regulations cannot govern. Perhaps the most important aspect of personal development for helping or serving others is a sense of humility, the sense that whatever happens is finally not up to you alone.

I think there should be a concept such as mastery in the helping professions. Zen offers an interesting analogy. Monks must complete their first training, which lasts ten years, in the monastery. Their next ten-year training, which has no rules to it, begins when they leave the monastery and enter the world. This informal training has no set ending; rather, at the end of the second ten-year period, the master sits with the monk and somehow knows whether or not the monk has become a master by the way in which she drinks tea, which is symbolic of how she lives Zen.

The public is only aware of its need for training and competence, not for mastery. It notices if a helper is more or less in order. It creates ethical codes based upon the right to live and an interest in maintaining sanity. These codes support the conventions of society and break down in unknown, mysterious areas. You need to go beyond our present definitions of health, life, and sanity and include your personal development as a requirement for helping other people. Otherwise you only serve society in its present form and not the spirit of the future. You need the sense of the spirit upon which everything rests. And you need the old concept of a mastery that can be attained only through innerwork, congruence, and luck.

In lieu of such mastery concepts, the doubts, fears, and insecurities of people who are growing into the helping professions become their personal tests and the regulations that inner development imposes. Your occasional sense of inferiority is not just a personal problem, but an essential aspect of personal growth. At every stage of development, you doubt and test yourself, not only because of the increasing complexity of the challenges, but because you need the sense of doubt to remain open to change and the spirit. Study is never enough. You must develop attitudes and skills that change as the overall consciousness of the world transforms.

Test by Power

Finally, you arrive at the surprising conclusion that your personal development is not up to you alone, but depends upon what is happening in our world. Thus, when don Juan doubts that Castaneda should be an apprentice, he conducts a test in which the spirit is the examiner. In this case, the spirit examiner is what don Juan calls Mescalito. Castaneda must encounter this deity by taking the mind-altering drug mescaline. Don Juan is trying to discover if the spirit, or what he calls power, will allow Castaneda to continue his apprenticeship. Is the spirit in favor of Castaneda pursuing the ways of the warrior?

Fate has it that Castaneda develops a strong magical bond to a dog he meets while in the drug-induced state. Don Juan accepts this numinous interaction during the drug trip as a sign that the apprenticeship must continue, despite his reservations concerning his apprentice's apparent superficiality. But now Castaneda must learn more than hunting. He must learn the ways of the warrior.

Power tests not only the student but also the teacher. A sensitive teacher understands that he grows with his clients or students. Fate binds us all, transforming what is defined as a healing process into a teacher-apprentice relationship, even if neither teacher nor apprentice is prepared. The client's projections onto the teacher need to be understood not only as parts of the learner's inner life to be integrated but also as hints about how the teacher must grow.

I remember how one of my training analysts understood my dreams. When he appeared as a god in my dreams, he always interpreted his image as a part of me. But he also spoke personally about his hopes of becoming more than he was, for he always had doubts about himself. Naturally, I thought he was God. But then, when I told him that I had seen him in my dreams in a negative light, he would describe himself as that negative person and encourage me to react to him as such, leaving it to me to find out if and how I was negative to my-self. His modesty was a model I am still trying to emulate.

The Warriors

Nature herself sets up special dream or druglike tests as trainings to determine which learner-teacher pairs are meant to go all the way together. Some pairs are meant to become the types of facilitators who are immaculate hunters. In these cases, the learning facilitator and the learner develop powerful hunting awareness and skills. These hunters prepare systems that identify and explain experiences, dreams, and world problems. They seek out, identify, support, or shoot down aspects of unconsciousness for others.

Hunters do not seem meant to leave their framework of given methods and routines in order to consciously identify with experiences. Don Juan differentiates hunters from warriors and says that the decision as to who becomes a hunter and who becomes a warrior is not up to us. Only an important omen can foretell it.

The hunter searches, annihilates, and integrates inner and outer events while staying in normal reality, but the warrior is different. She connects directly and experientially with these conflicts and events. The warrior, as you shall soon see, lives the dreamingbody.

Phases of Development

Centuries of working with altered states of consciousness have allowed shamanic teachers to describe stages of development in awareness training. Don Juan mentions various phases of relating to the world besides as hunter or warrior. These are as the so-called average man, the sorcerer, and the seer.

The average person never leaves the domain of consensus reality but dwells within the walls of the ordinary world; he never touches the perimeter of the unconscious, secondary awareness, or the unknown. The sorcerer leaves the ordinary world of consciousness and derives strength from the powers she finds at the outer perimeter. She lets herself be possessed by secondary processes, the experiences beyond this perimeter. But like the average person, the sorcerer is possessed by her reality.

People with a calling to become facilitators, analysts, therapists, or teachers become hunters. Some hunters become sorcerers. They love dwelling in the unconscious and resist viewing their findings in the light of consensus reality. They love hypnosis, secret medicines, and magical interventions and avoid direct confrontations in order to transform ordinary consciousness. They satisfy our occasional need for an immediate solution to suffering.

The hunters and sorcerers I know always seem to be fighting with one another. Hunters feel that sorcerers do not take consciousness seriously enough, but rather regress to archaic history. Hunters love everyday reality and stay there. Sorcerers see hunters as insufficiently mystical and irrational. They insist that hunters should have more relationship to power, rather than only supporting everyday reality.

The seer, on the other hand, is all and none of these types. He is the fluid individual who can act like an average person, analyze like a hunter, dive in like a warrior, dwell in the other world like a sorcerer, and laugh at all the other types, because he knows that they are all just ways of being, that none is any better than the rest.

Who becomes which type is not a personal choice. You need all of these abilities. Furthermore, you are all of these types at one time or another. The relationship you have to a momentary process is a matter of personal style and fate. Anyone and everyone is an average person and also a bit of a seer, a hunter, and a warrior. But who identifies as a shaman depends upon dreams and heritage.

According to creation myths and shamanic stories, every living thing has the chance for immortality.[2] Who picks up on this chance to transcend the everyday consciousness of the ordinary person and when or how deeply you succeed at this depends upon special conditions. Thus, hunter, sorcerer, warrior, or seer are not fixed states of being to which you must associate yourself forever. Rather each is a stage on the road to freedom and the perpetuation of awareness.

Of course, you may tend to behave more like one state than another. If you identify with your intelligence, you will learn to become a great hunter and stay there. But if you are unusual in some way, you may manage, over a long period of time and through tremendous suffering, to become a warrior or a seer.

Dreaming

Dreaming is a route to power for a warrior. The difference between a hunter and a warrior is that the warrior seeks and is touched by power, while the hunter knows little about it.[3] The hunter catches sight of the unknown and eats it while remaining in ordinary reality, the known world. Like many psychotherapists today, the hunter tries to explain the power of processes. Today we speak of the unconscious, childhood experiences, biological conditions, dream figures, complexes, neuroses, resistances, archetypes, and abuse issues.

The hunter explains while the warrior dives in. The warrior experiences power. She allows power to explain itself by moving her to dance, cry, meditate, and yell.

"Power" is a Native American term for the vitalizing and electrifying experience of secondary processes. For shamans, the central avenue to power is dreaming, which is much more than remembering images during sleep. It is even more than lucid dreaming, in which you remain conscious while asleep. Dreaming is something like Jung's active imagination, where the dreamer encounters dream experiences on paper, through dance, or in her head, in the form of inner dialogues or visualizations.

The shaman's dreaming, however, involves the sense of energy and does not revolve simply around insight or the improvement of everyday life. Through noticing, identifying, differentiating, confronting, and following unusual secondary processes as they appear at any moment, shamans have always derived a vitality and renewed sense of themselves. That is why shamans and healers today give you the impression that they are connected to something infinite and ungraspable.

This reminds me of an uncanny meeting I had with an unusual man in the high mountains of eastern Oregon. The man had entered the run-down cafe where Amy and I were having breakfast one morning on a road off the beaten track. Unlike other people, he looked down at the floor and walked slowly and surely, as if in a partial trance. I was immediately attracted to his centeredness and, after saying hello, asked him who he was. He responded by asking what I was doing. I told him I was just finishing this book on shamanism and asked if he knew what that was all about. "Oh yes," he replied, "I am a Native American Indian and lead sweat lodges myself in the mountains."

What a pleasure, but what a shock I had. In any case, it seems that studying dreaming connects you to it just as training in dreaming leads to power and traditionally occurs mainly in the wilderness. The core of the shaman's learning is the experience of secondary processes. Remember that primary processes are experiences that are closer to your awareness, events and images with which you identify or which you intend to create. Secondary processes are further from awareness and are more surprising. They can be awesome, terrifying, or confusing. They may be auditory hallucinations, sudden visions, or nighttime apparitions. They can be headaches, pains, or unpredictable movements. Relationship problems that you cannot solve and unremitting world problems are all secondary.

Metaphorically speaking, all of these processes happen during the night, that is, during the darkness of the day. It feels as if they are hurled at you or at least as if they have been invited without your consent. According to shamans, such events must be handled with the tools of dreaming, which means going consciously into these experiences and getting to know them from within. After you have learned to hunt and think about yourself, you study your behavior and dreams and begin to comprehend others. The next step is to leave the banks of the river from which you have been observing and get into the stream.

It is easy to describe dreaming but difficult to consciously step into the stream and cocreate life with it. Before you can abandon yourself to the unknown, you need an immense amount of inner control and security. You may also need a model of someone else who manages to do it. That is why shamans have always learned from helpful spirits or old master shamans. Without the help of such figures, you tend to remain for long periods of time with the primary processes, as if at the port on the mainland from which you sail.

It takes so much energy to master the doings of this world that you may repress secondary dimensions of your experience. Therefore, you must "set up" these secondary dimensions. For this reason, don Juan teaches his apprentice to begin dreaming by setting up dreams. He warns against simply falling into dreaming and advises approaching dreaming consciously and willfully. Unlike the ordinary person, who is periodically swamped by moods, illnesses, and relationship problems, the warrior willfully establishes a knowledge of dreamlike events. He deliberately decides when and how to approach them, in a disciplined manner.

The shaman warns that opening up to power and learning to dream are dangerous tasks that could lead to death. If you are unfamiliar with dream and body processes, you are likely to find this a bit exaggerated. How can learning the warrior's art be a matter of life and death? Why were analysts who followed Jung always afraid that people would go crazy if they went into the "unconscious" too early?

The answer to both of these questions is that allowing yourself to become unconsciously submerged causes you to "flip," to change personalities, and, hence, to die metaphorically. This happens every time you get into a bad mood. When you enter the unknown without preparation, you become possessed by moods, spirits, emotions, complexes, and symptoms. From morning until night, you worry about something happening or not happening and about your health and welfare.

A reader once wrote to me about these problems after he had tried to follow suggestions in my book *Working with the Dreamingbody*. He had followed the instructions and tried to get behind the creative energy of his headaches. He was like a hunter making the first attempts at being a warrior. He first felt the pain in his head and noticed that it was like something striking out at him. He picked up the energy, became the striking figure himself, and hit a pillow. His headache improved, but before he knew what had happened, he had unconsciously identified with his father, who had violently abused him as a child.

Then, instead of simply becoming more assertive, this man became abusive to everyone around him. In this way, he drowned in his process; he metaphorically died. He became intoxicated by this new altered state of consciousness. The state had been repressed until then and could only appear in a symptom. But as he worked on himself alone, he lost access to his ordinary personality and became possessed by an inner figure. He abandoned himself to secondary processes, but not in a controlled way. Such minor deaths are errors that are part of the shaman's path.

On the other hand, if you do nothing but notice secondary processes and avoid them, they tend to amplify themselves and become destructive. Left to themselves, certain secondary processes, such as aches and pains, become body problems and finally annihilate your primary identity by making you sick. Secondary processes that are ignored turn chaotic and chronic; they confuse your communication to others and destroy your health and well-being.

In this way, your hunter's trim and orderly life is at stake while you hunt for power. The primary process of the hunter—that is, your respect, reserve, and exacting nature—must not disappear when you contact experiences in altered states of consciousness. You must stay sober even while you are in these altered states of consciousness.

When you are a warrior, dreaming is the essence of reality, because you can learn to act deliberately during such times by selecting secondary processes that lead to power. You can touch these events and use them, whereas in an ordinary dream you do not act consciously, but are swept along with events.

Learning to dream is not haphazard but active and deliberate. You consciously intervene with spontaneous experiences, combining altered states of consciousness with wakeful interventions and, above all, noticing which are primary and close to consciousness and which are secondary and far away. The warrior senses something unknown to her and consciously decides to use her second attention to explore it. She feels her way into processes, selecting events and experiences according to the energy in them. The events that are strangest and furthest from awareness, the most unearthly secondary processes, are the ones with the most power.

Perhaps you can follow me best by actually trying this while reading. Set up dreaming in the sense of finding something that is happening right now at the periphery of your awareness. Choose those events that are most unusual. Focus on them. Then amplify, strengthen, and support their signals in an effort to unfold their secrets. If they are body problems, enter into feeling them. If they are sudden fantasies, remain with visions. If they are unusual movements or sounds, go with them.

Remain acutely aware of what is happening. If you find yourself backing off from experiences, you may have reached an edge, and your personal history may be holding you up. Notice this edge—that is, your hesitations and resistances to what is happening—and consciously decide whether to progress or to turn back. In ordinary dreaming and imaginations, impasses or edges usually go unnoticed. You avoid them by changing subjects, waking up, or becoming distracted.

Power, the mind-altering, energizing, and enlightening experience of your secondary process, is not entirely explainable in terms of your individual personality or the specific content of a message. You always experience life in terms of your personal self, yet the energy and timing behind processes are uncontrollable. Energy comes to you when it will, as if you were its channel. You can only join power consciously and try to use its energy to stay on the path, the river of dreaming. The nature of this power remains a mystery whose final explanation may never come.

Shamans give apprentices special tasks during dreaming in order for the apprentices to remain lucid. Don Juan gives Castaneda the task of looking at his hands in his dreams as the first step in learning how to dream. There is nothing special about looking at your hands, but looking at anything in a dream is a way of remembering your ordinary self while in the midst of unconsciousness. To find your hands in your dreams is to remain wakeful in the midst of dreaming and everyday slumber, your normal waking states of unconsciousness.

If you notice that you are in the midst of a secondary process, you can "wake up," that is, you can apply your second attention and complete it. Otherwise, you simply dream and get enmeshed within that dream. Then you are in a bad mood. Consciously dreaming means remembering your whole self, no matter what state you are in: remembering your good-heartedness even when you are enraged, remembering the meaning of life even when you are depressed, remembering cold soberness even when you are drunk. Dreaming or working with secondary processes is best when you are in these two separate states of mind at the same time. You dream but are also aware of your ordinary self.

My brother, Carl, told me an amusing story that illustrates this point. One of his meditation teachers was doing an apprenticeship in India and found himself in the deepest and most magnificent of trances at the ashram. Just then, his guru walked by and abruptly interrupted his Nirvana to ask him to show the ashram to an American tourist who had just arrived.

The guru was not impressed by the teacher's absorption in Nirvana.

The message in the guru's action was that you should not forget yourself in an altered state of consciousness. If you do, the tools you have learned will not be available to you. You should have your ecstatic experiences and also disidentify from them. The first step in working on yourself alone is to realize that you are the observer as well as the participant. Choose when to identify with and when to disidentify with the trip. You must remember your whole self even when you are dreaming.

There are many methods for distinguishing yourself from the processes you are working with in order to resist possession. One is to bring your ordinary, everyday problems and issues with you into your inner experiences. If you remember your ordinary self while in the midst of an altered state, not only do you avoid floating away, but you can enable the transformation of your everyday personality to take place. This is watching your hands while dreaming.

Metaskills

Regardless of the method you use, the feelings you have about unusual experiences seem to determine the success of your experiences. Not only are the skills and techniques important, but the feelings with which you use the techniques—what Amy calls metaskills—are also crucial.

The most useful and special metaskill is a form of heartfulness: compassion for yourself and loving interest in the things you experience. I have no idea how to learn or teach this feeling, though I know that it is more important than any of the other paraphernalia or skills.

This detached heartfulness is powerful in your dealing with the most seductive of all trance states: ordinary reality. How wonderful but how difficult it is to remember that you are an infinite being interested in life and death during everyday times, especially during difficult moments or concerning relationship issues.

In such special moments when you remember your whole self, you can go deep into the mundaneness of ordinary reality and enjoy its mystery. Waking up entails remembering your whole self in the midst of trance states and problems and making sense out of them. It does not mean being without problems.

Everyone undergoes the cycle of discovering, being fatigued, sleeping, and reawakening. The warrior, however, tries to break this cycle by remembering his entire self at all times. When he is in the world of daily activity, he is at the same time on a mountaintop, just as when he is asleep, he is awake. The skill is an ability to pick up on secondary processes, but the metaskill is compassion for yourself and the experience.

In dreaming, it is crucial to notice what is happening and also to sustain the view of your experience. In the martial arts, fighting is a skill, but love for the universe that organizes that encounter is a metaskill. The metaskill in the martial encounter allows everyone to win. Likewise, processwork has skills in it, as Amy has shown; the compassion or ruthlessness with which the work is done is the metaskill that defines the work.

Thus the skill of dreaming is the second attention, but compassion for yourself and your experience are the metaskills. You notice and work with power. Metaskills have no pointers to them. The method of sustaining a secondary process once it comes up depends upon awareness and amplification, but your final ability at this depends upon your love for the unpredictable. To work with the unknown, some combination of respect, ruthlessness, courage, and cuddling is necessary. These metaskills may be different from your attitudes in ordinary meditation procedures.

One of the important feelings or beliefs behind sustaining an unusual process is the sense that once that process comes up, it will carry you into the adventure of becoming whole. If you have questions, the process will be its own answer. If you are troubled by something, it will solve itself without your plans. Jung said that a dream is its own best interpretation. Similarly, Wilhelm Reich's theory was that the body will correct itself. Pantanjali, one of the earliest Yoga teachers and writers, said, "Yoga teaches Yoga." Once you begin with your second attention, the processes that you experience become your instructors.

When you slip and do something that seems foolish, then, instead of hating yourself for the error, try honoring the unknown in your own nature that made the "mistake"; love the mistake and encourage it to unfold further. If a friend says one thing but does another, befriend the "other," but don't forget the friend. The metaskills of dreaming will inhibit you from criticizing your own and other's unconsciousness and encourage you instead to enter deeper into it. Rather than neglecting body symptoms and accidents, welcome them. If you climb aboard such energies, life is richer for all. Create symptoms, don't just experience them. When dreams befuddle you, hold to the dreaming process.

The shaman in you understands power as a love for the unusual, a love that brings everything to life. Love for the absurd is a transformative metaskill that turns anything and anybody into gold. Worship not the object, but the spirit that animates it; not the content, but the creative element in the background.

Anything you see, hear, feel, or relate to is real, whether or not it can be repeated. If you suddenly fantasize something, then its pattern is there; it is trying to happen. It is your life energy—your greatest, perhaps your only, possession.

Thus, that animal in the throes of death is real, because this was our apprentice himself and his own routines that were dying. This is real. The lesson of the little stick is the following: If you want to be a hunter, then you must have the skills to notice when something unusual is happening. You must study that thing. But if you want to be a warrior, you must have second attention; not only must you catch sight of power or feel it, you must honor and befriend its energy.

Without such an attitude, every time something uncontrollable happens, you think you made it up yourself and unwittingly kill life-giving power by not noticing and discovering the mysterious. This attitude provokes and disturbs nature, which then reacts. I remember a man who suffered from "severe hallucinations," as they were called. At that time in Switzerland, drugs for inhibiting hallucinations were not used as much as they are today, and seeing a client in the midst of a schizophrenic episode was not all that unusual. In any case, my client was now lost in overwhelming visions, swamped by unpredictable and terrifying monsters.

At one point in our work, he cried out, "I am the monster from the mountains," and lifted my chair, with me in it, from the floor. I got scared, froze, and fell into the dreaming world. I insisted that he disidentify with what was happening—basically for my own benefit. I yelled back, "I am Arny, therapist from Zurich, ready to eat lunch!" Naturally, the monster was not the least bit impressed and began to lift a second chair.

My first attempt to stop the act had been a failure, but luckily I remembered my whole self and thought that this must be the moment to sustain the image of the monster and befriend it. So I took a chance and yelled, "Hey there! I'm glad you've arrived. I'll bet you have come to help my client with his everyday life. Nice to have you with me today. You sure are powerful!" The monster paused for a moment and seemed to listen.

It screamed back, "Your client is a wimp, a weakling who is afraid of his own mother!" whereupon my client broke down and cried.

The man, now in a more or less normal state of consciousness, seemed to forget his hallucinations and begged me to help him defend himself against his mother, who had evidently sexually abused him when he was a child.

"Remember the powerful monster," I pleaded to the man in his normal state. "Do you really believe in that monster?" my client asked. "Yes," I said, "and if you intend to remain sane, I recommend that you believe in the monster as well. Otherwise, it will get angry at all of us." The man replied that believing in that stuff had a powerful consequence. "Now I'll have to learn to defend myself!"

EXERCISES

1. Write a brief personal history. How do you identify yourself right now? In what tasks are you involved? Are you a man or a woman? With what race, religion, or group do you identify, if any? Are you single or in the midst of a family?

2. Ask if nature will allow you to experiment with being a warrior for a few minutes. If you are uncertain, throw a coin, ask the *I Ching*, or imagine asking a wise inner dream figure if you can at least be a hunter.

3. Now your path is open, and you must go further. Use your first attention, and hunt for power. Notice what is happening, and check for something unpredictable in or around yourself. Don't take long to do this.

4. Go ahead and catch that unpredictable thing. Now use your second attention. Hold this unusual experience or event. Focus upon it with your seeing, hearing, feeling, and moving—as if it required the greatest respect and honor. Hold your attention on this, carefully giving it time to live and reveal itself. Love it.

5. If you are unable to hold your second attention on the unusual thing, the reason may be that you are attached to your personal history. Go back and study what you wrote about yourself in the first part of this exercise. Ask yourself if this history is essential to you in the moment or if you can afford to drop it for a short time. Drop your history as a warrior would and allow yourself to observe and experience the unpredictable thing once again. Begin by just dropping this history for a moment.

6. Follow the event or experience and pretend you are the force, energy, or power behind it. Notice how your body and mind change.

7. Don't forget your "hands," your everyday consciousness. Ask yourself how and if this force could be used to transform everyday reality and your personal history.

8. Now travel in the stream of events and let your dreaming carry you.

ARNOLD MINDELL

CHAPTER 7

THE ALLY

As you develop in your ability to hunt and dream, typical barriers appear, inhibiting awareness. These barriers are classical edges going by many names. According to don Juan, they may be called clarity, fear, power, or old age. To attain any degree of self-knowledge and fluidity, you must confront these barriers.

When you start complaining about how weird everything is getting, you may be meeting the barrier called clarity. The need for clarity and understanding blocks your perception and makes you ignore aspects of life that seem irrational, illogical, or strange. Clarity tells you that what is happening is too strange to be real or that it is just plain crazy. Clarity, however, is only an edge, a barrier to be overcome.

I met clarity for the first time in Mombasa, Kenya, on the eastern Indian Ocean, when I was sitting on the floor with Amy in the bush hut of our Girami healers. Our healers, a shaman couple, went into trances and performed herbal and surgical healings. I can still remember vividly the strange dances and trances this couple did, especially the woman, who screamed and rolled around on the earthen floor. The combination of their exotic language, the strange herbal potions we had to drink, the surgical healings they performed for the other villagers present, and the woman's telepathic ability to visualize my "enemies" back home was so utterly foreign to me that clarity came forth to block my experiences for a few minutes. My mind refused to participate in the ceremony.

My studies in shamanism and anthropology helped reduce the barrier set up by my unconscious need for clarity. I finally decided to allow my occasional experiences of telepathy—which I had never been able to understand—be my guide. I let go and allowed the effect of the mystery to lead my body along its way. The ceremony took hours. Our healers stripped us and reclothed us as Africans in order to initiate us into their mysteries. Their love and the awe I experienced during those two days and nights enabled me to get around the barrier of clarity.

Clarity no longer binds me today; whenever someone wants to know what she is going to encounter in working on herself, I simply admit that I do not know. I can only say that she may want to know, but that the best way to discover what is on the other side is to hold reservations at bay long enough to let processes themselves disclose their own nature. Bring clarity along. Do not fight it, but use it to define as much of the unknown as possible.

When you start worrying about security, fear is at your doorstep. Fear is a difficult enemy because, even if you are using your sense of clarity, the imagined danger of the unknown worries you. You are afraid of being hurt, run down, or killed. Fear is usually wrapped up with the loss of identity. If security is crucial to you, the unknown feels threatening. Therefore, it is helpful to work on erasing personal history and realizing that you are ultimately more than your identity. Losing yourself for short periods of time is not the worst thing that could happen. It could even be a relief.

When you accept and respect your fears, you are no longer in danger of dying at the hands of the unknown; instead, you participate in your own transformation. If you relax your previous identity before it is eliminated, you can meet uncanny forces that are stronger than you are and learn new things. Finally, you feel stronger.

But when your self-confidence begins to irritate everyone around you, power may be a problem. After you get past clarity and fear, the problem of power looms up. Power is truly a most troublesome enemy, for you attain it without even realizing it. When you assume that the experiences you have are the ones that others should have, when you think your way is more or less the only way, you are troubled by power. Power is especially troublesome if you have had big experiences. From your limited but incredible experience of the unknown, you make maps of the path you have taken and believe others must follow the same route. When power overcomes you, you act wise, have answers for everything, and feel insulted and defensive if others do not agree. You interpret, advise, explain, and warn, as if you, not nature, were the teacher.

Perhaps the worst side of power is inferiority. You have such immense images of who you ought to be that anything less than those images depresses you. Thus, when you are not inflated, you are depressed and miserable because you yourself cannot follow the golden path you have determined for everyone. Power is a dreadful enemy; it makes you lose your humor and become increasingly depressed, serious, and bossy. Power seduces you into thinking that you know what should happen. The truth of the matter is that no one has any more power than anyone else, and you have only that power which is given to you in any moment.

Everyone remembers their moments of power and can recall what they have been through. The voices and messages of your way were meaningful to you and the world you lived in at that moment. But times change, and the power of that moment and its message may mean nothing in the next moment. Your chance for remaining connected to the uncanny forces in nature depends upon remaining open to them and being able to experience one moment after the next.

To get around power, try accepting it. It must be present, because you are still not following your own rules and regulations. If you try to use your power on that part of yourself that needs a good kick, it might transform into laughter. Then you will realize that you are your own worst apprentice—but who cares? Finally, you start relaxing, and before you know it, nothing seems to matter.

After you have worked with fear, clarity, and power, you meet one of the most difficult barriers of all: old age. Old age is truly subtle and can occur at any age. It seems to me that old age begins with a feeling of detachment. Then, before you know it, you get bored, and suddenly old age is upon you.

After you have overcome power, when connection to the world and importance to others are no longer interesting, the greatest conflict arises. Why go on with life at all? What for? Suddenly you are not merely enlightened but exhausted. You feel you have had enough and done more than was needed. How about some vacation? Why not let everyone else care for that crazy world? This kind of old age is not detachment but a subtle and chronic depression that hides a crucial insight. You must truly die to become yourself; even your detachment must die. It, too, is just another state of mind. The exhausting kind of detachment is apathy that arises when compulsion is past.

If the sense of old age leads to a metaphorical death, however, emptiness can turn to creativity, and you can start to develop a beginner's mind again. Even a near-death experience can be a new beginning. Of the people I have worked with who were near death, everyone who was not too severely brain damaged to speak after returning from a comatose state has behaved as if life were continuing. Many have said they wanted to work on themselves. I recall how my mother told me with a smile, just before she died, that she was coming to Zurich to study. Peter, the man I report on in my book *Coma, Key to Awakening,* said just before his death that I should take care of his wife and children and that he was going to go on working with me.

Old age, it seems, is only an enemy when you need to die. Once you have died, you can go on living more fully than before.

The Ally

One of the differences between a warrior and a hunter is that a warrior has an ally. This is the mark of the shaman. Once you have learned how to hunt and have learned to deal with some of your barriers, a next important step is to develop a relationship to an ally.

According to Eliade, "A shaman is a man who has immediate, concrete experiences with gods and spirits; he sees them face to face, he talks with them, prays to them, implores them—but he does not 'control' more than a limited number of them."[1] Those gods and spirits, those allies most familiar to the shaman, are often dogs, bulls, colts, eagles, elk, or brown bears. The ally may be the spirit of a dead shaman, or it may be a minor celestial spirit. It may be called the "bush soul" in Australia or the "nagual" in Central America or Mexico.

To assist in his learning, the warrior must find himself either a magical inner guru or a teacher. The psychology behind this is that you need to realize and respect something besides your present identity as your teacher. The ally is a teacher that, while a friend of our ordinary mind, is the symbol or expression of an altered state of consciousness. The ally, you could say, is a bridge between the worlds. In shamanistic terms, becoming whole means finding your ally and asking it to help you find other lost or missing parts of your soul.

According to all shamans, the ally is a necessity, for it can help you understand things that other human beings could not possibly know. The ally can carry you beyond the boundaries of yourself and give you a sense of friendship and security in the world that ordinary life cannot give you.

The ally balances you and can give you a feeling of power when you experience yourself as weak. But it can also make you feel worthless when you are ambitious, ill when you want to govern life. The ally is impossible and dangerous; yet without it, life is empty. Without a conscious relationship to an ally, all you can do is search for altered states of consciousness by addicting yourself to foods or drugs.

Does the concept of the ally sound unfamiliar or strange to you? Remember your childhood teddy bear, which kept you company when things got rough? That toy bear was nice to you even when no one else was. Your dolls and stuffed animals were parental allies that showed you how to love and care for yourself when you faced the night alone. Or they were your child allies, doing things that were naughty and forbidden to you.

Not just the shaman, but everyone searches for imaginary friends, dream figures, and outer teachers to model for and guide them when life seems impossible. Such figures appear almost automatically when you must enter the river of dreams. Near death, you will probably be like others and suddenly notice already-dead parents or friends who appear to help you across the threshold into new dimensions. You experience parents and wise people who have died as superb allies, especially if you loved them.

Most adults forget their allies, but many have phases of searching for helpful outer teachers or inner spirits. Some pray to God. A shaman or seer must have familiars, beings that inspire and teach, speak in strange tongues, and educate about things that humans could not know.

Allies are a part of your personal psychology, but they seem to exist outside you as well. In fact, much of life may be organized by something like a guardian angel. While you are working at your tasks, you feel that you are doing them. However, when you look back, you may have the feeling that whatever you have done was done by a force other than yourself. Don't you sometimes feel as if you would never have the power or courage to accomplish certain jobs alone? You sense that something like a guiding light, a helpful angel, or an ally is behind your fate.

Allies may appear in dreams, fantasies, and body symptoms. Or they may appear first after an attack from a friend or in the midst of a difficult crisis. The most powerful allies impinge upon you. You want life to go in one direction, but unconscious energies go in another.

Most people I have worked with discover their most valuable allies as adults. Though I have known many people who have had allies, few like to speak much about their relationship to these figures, since it is such a deep and personal matter. Jesus was an ally of one of my healers. The ally of one of my favorite teachers was Jung. And Jung says in his autobiography that he spoke with several figures. The ancient wise figure he called Philemon was most helpful.

Testing the Ally

Before using their allies to help them journey into other worlds to find the soul or missing objects, shamans measure the value of their allies, considering coyotes and dogs to be less valuable than bears, for example.[2] The ally is a spirit that may have power but no intelligence, perseverance but no heart, wisdom but no feeling. The ally is not necessarily wise, whole, or complete by itself. Know your allies.

Shamans say that a person is no better than his ally. The problem is that few people know that they even have an ally. Most think they have no power at all, which really means that their powers are unconscious. Some people, however, have always had something like a spirit helper.

Do you have a spirit helper? What is your ally like? Do you have a figure or object or body feeling from which you seek guidance? Did your ally first appear during a crisis, when you could go no further? What happened to you then? That special help you once got—the wisdom, strength, or cunning— might be or have been your ally. Do you still use this figure? Get to know your deepest self, this ally, and meet it. Learn about its strengths and weaknesses.

If your ally is a coyote, you tend to be like that animal; you might be liar or a cheat. Don't be naive about yourself. Some allies, perhaps all allies, inflate you. True, they give you what you do not have in the moment. But they may also make you act and feel wiser, tougher, better, or more enlightened than others. They may even make you feel sick and worthless if you are too ambitious. The nature of the ally's power causes these effects.

Many allies, even dead spiritual teachers and guides, cannot help you much with everyday life because they have little interest in mundane reality. These allies look interesting in dreams, but if untested, they take you into fantastic realms or transpersonal flights of wonder, avoiding banal, everyday human problems.

Sometimes, in fact, don Juan's comments sound like the voice of his ally. This may be why many of Castaneda's readers thought that don Juan was only a part of the apprentice's imagination. Nevertheless, don Juan (or the figure called don Juan, whom Castaneda may have put together from many different people) has the sound knowledge of someone with a great deal of real experience in differentiating unusual and altered states of consciousness. Don Juan is even able to look carefully at his own teacher. His teacher's ally was the devil's weed, which made him act too powerfully, don Juan says.

Some communities differentiate shamans into so-called black and white types, depending upon the nature of their allies and the kind of magic they are able to do. Don Juan compares two allies' experiences he calls "the devil's weed" and "the little smoke," both of which could be induced with drugs. He prefers the experiences of the little smoke, which leads to detachment. He tells Castaneda, who naturally falls in love with the power of the devil's weed, that there is no longer any need for the weed. Don Juan dislikes power. In earlier times, he says, Native Americans could perform phenomenal deeds and were admired, feared, and respected for their power. But now, he says, the power of the devil's weed is no longer needed.[3]

If you think psychologically, you can understand the experiences of the weed and the smoke induced by drugs as normal states of mind that you usually go through without identifying them as such. The people around you, however, notice when you are possessed by the weed or the smoke.

When you feel disempowered during certain phases of life, you seek more of the weed's power. But looking for such power is only a momentary phase of development, for it leads to unsustainable relationships and a community in which everyone beats up everyone else. In any case, it seems to me that whether your ally has the characteristic of the devil's weed or of the little smoke is a matter of where you are in your development. Early on, you need power and must grow stronger to live in the world. Later on, however, you grow tired of being forceful and need a new kind of spirit helper, something like the little smoke that brings you heart and patience.

The Devil's Weed

You can sense when someone is possessed by the weed because she cannot let go of who she is and what she has produced. How many teachers do you know who, perhaps like yourself, are possessed by their own systems and become blind to everything else? Yet, according to shamans, there is no final judgment about this. The only crucial thing is to be as objective about your ally as possible.

Be careful about being seduced by your ally's flattery. If your ally is like the weed, then your inner deity seduces you and makes you ambitious. You can't stand your friends and colleagues who are doing as well as or better than you are. You can't wait to put them down.

The most typical characteristic of those who become addicted to the devil's weed is that they suffer from having been hurt and constantly fight off a sense of unworthiness. They want to be stronger for fear of weakness. They seem to be particularly susceptible to being liked or disliked by others. If they lose a friend, they are not simply jealous, but violent. Perhaps the real weakness they suffer is a lack of compassion for themselves or others. Instead of developing heart, they get tough and are attracted to tough people, which in turn makes them feel even less loved.

While you scarcely realize that you have been seduced by the devil's weed, that ally makes you a prisoner and addicts you to compliments. When you don't get enough compliments, you become, without the weed, wimpy and hateful.

An example of someone possessed by the devil's weed comes to mind. An unhappy man who had been too gentle for years suffered from a lack of aggressiveness and definitiveness. He found himself becoming more and more militant. As he investigated his new powers, he became inadvertently aggressive and began to disturb everyone around him. Slowly, he came to feel tougher and smarter than others and began to teach others what he felt they needed to know, even though they hadn't asked for enlightenment. Finally, one day, he sensed that something was not right and asked me, in his powerful fashion, to "mow" him down. I didn't want to do this because I liked him and because I did not have the power he thought I had. It was his weed telling me what to do.

In any case, there was no way out. I implored him in vain to find his lost humility again. Finally, he pressed me beyond all of my limits. I lost my temper and mowed him down. "Shut up and change!" I yelled. Though my explosion had a great effect, I felt terrible for having acted roughly, even if only for a moment. Immediately after I was forceful, I begged forgiveness for having been tough on him. My sadness must have touched him, for he changed on the spot. Several days after the confrontation, he told me that he realized he had been possessed by power and, of all things, thanked me.

This person was magnificent. Not everyone could change so quickly. He realized he had been possessed by power, he had the humility to change, and he said he wanted to learn more about himself. I must admit that during times when I have been possessed by the weed I have had no humility. The problem with spirit possession is that those who are in it never experience it as such. When you are possessed, you are moved out of your own house, so to speak. You never think you are possessed by an ally because you are so impressed with feeling something so powerful.

The feelings of power or worthlessness impress you so immensely that you lack the distance to see that this state of mind could ruin your life if untested. If you awaken and interact with the weed, however, you have the freedom to use its power as needed and then drop it. You can have access to the devil's weed without being possessed by it. You may accomplish amazing feats of strength but will not identify with your accomplishments afterward.

In all of my life I remember only one person who has had such access to the weed's power and yet been free from it. This was Barbara Hannah, a teacher of mine who was in her eighties when I met her in Zurich in the 1960s. I will never forget her using the power of the devil's weed one day during a class she was giving. An obnoxious class participant went up to her after a lecture she had given and asked an irritating question. I was standing between my impossible classmate and Ms. Hannah when the classmate insisted on getting her foolish question answered.

Ms. Hannah, to my great surprise, let out an incredible hissing sound, like that of a snake. My classmate, who had seemed inflated to me at the time, turned pale and almost collapsed. Ms. Hannah responded suddenly by sweetly and quietly asking the shocked student if she had forgotten her question. "Poor one," Ms. Hannah said, "you look pale. Shall I get someone to take you home?" I could not believe the change in that dreadful classmate. The next time I saw her, she actually looked attractive, and Ms. Hannah was as nice as could be to her. She was not possessed by the weed but had used her power as an ally to bring about useful change.

The Little Smoke

The power of the little smoke is very different from that of the weed. While the weed requires power or strength, the smoke challenges you to have heart and to think of eternity, of the next century. If your ally is the smoke, then you worry about everyone's future, not only your own.

There is something noble about this ally; those with it seem to have pure hearts. The smoke neither loves nor hates; it puts you in a mood that enables you to step out of the circle of emotions. In Tibetan terms, the smoke is the ally that gets you off the Karmic wheel. In fact, though the weed and the smoke are named after hallucinogenic drugs, the moods they arouse within you are in everyone, all the time.

The strength of the heart, regardless of its manifestation, frees you from the turmoil and commotion of daily life; it helps you to laugh at your own and others' foolishness. Even more important, the smoke gives you the capacity to persevere when things seem tough or when odds are against you. The weed may give you the strength to defend yourself in difficult situations, but the smoke gives you something more: detachment from the fight. It reminds you that what is happening is only momentary and that everything—especially people—changes like the seasons.

While the weed makes you feel responsible for everything that happens, the smoke reminds you that your job is to ride the powerful waves of change, not to create them. Both allies are the metaskills you unconsciously use when working on yourself. While the weed tries to push and change your behavior, the smoke encourages you to go deeper into it. The weed wants permanent solutions and resolutions; the smoke recommends seeing clearly. With the smoke as your ally, you can accept weakness. The smoke presses you to measure events by eternal standards. It wants to know if your life is sufficiently human.

Though the attitude of little smoke is usually associated with wisdom, age, and detachment, many young people also have the spirit of the little smoke. I remember once running near Mombasa on the eastern Indian Ocean. The weather suddenly changed, and it began to pour so heavily that I had to seek shelter in a cave on the beach. To my surprise, sitting on his heels in that cave was a young Kenyan man. He smiled at my shock at seeing him sitting there so quietly.

The man said his name was Amani, which means "peace" in Swahili. Amani's parents had named him after the Africans took Kenya from the British twenty-some years ago. Amani said that I and most white people had a more difficult time than the Africans because most white people are always striving for something, going somewhere, needing something. He said that the Africans had learned to be absolutely happy over long periods of time with almost nothing.

Amani was a man of peace. He had found his own little smoke, so to speak, and I did too for that moment in that cave on the eastern Indian Ocean.

The Body as Ally

I have had various allies. After completing my studies in physics and in Jungian psychology, I found myself constantly talking to the same two allies for years, a female and a male spirit. The potency of my relationships to these figures showed up constantly in my fantasies, dreams, and meditations.

Then I learned dreambodywork, and I found these visions in the feelings of my body. I learned to consult my body as an ally, asking it what to do in certain situations. I spent months trying to follow the unpredictable nature of my physical sensations instead of changing them. I went through unusual experiences while hiking for days in the Swiss Alps. Up until that time, the early 1970s, I had suffered from constant colds and flus. But following my dreamingbody helped me with this problem. I developed enormous sensitivity to the cold and learned to intuit the wind and breezes before they even seemed to blow. I would sometimes find myself running, as if for my life, as my body taught me how to hide behind trees or large rocks whenever a little breeze came up. I enjoyed playing with the breeze, rocks, and trees, but I also appreciated the resulting freedom this gave me from the flu. In fact, I did not get a cold or sore throat for many years thereafter.

Though an ally is a source of wisdom that may appear in your visions or auditory hallucinations, it can also appear in other channels. This power can be found as the force behind spontaneous dance or movement, in the wise directions of given body sensations, or in the sense of awesomeness in the wilderness.

What is the connection between body wisdom and ally figures? Whereas the names you give your allies usually refer to visual pictures or stories, like the weed or little smoke, the appearance of the ally in the body is more difficult to formulate in words. To understand the wisdom of your body, ask yourself what drives your body. What does the "push" or fatigue behind your body feel like? What does it look like?

Ask yourself what part of your body feels wisest. Try doing this right now. Scan your body and feel the answer. What does your body wisdom feel like? Feel it and try to make an image that corresponds to the feeling. What does this picture look like? See this picture located in that part of your body. If you have a question, ask it of this part of your body, this ally. Ask it lovingly, and wait, feel, or listen for an answer. Or let this wise part move you just now.

Various cultures locate the seat of consciousness and wisdom in different places of the body: the bottom of the spine, the solar plexus, the heart, the neck, the eyes, the top of the head. The important thing for you is to consider the possibility that your greatest wisdom may be located at a certain point in your body.

Thus, allies appear as feelings, dreams, and spirit figures, perceived in visual, auditory, and body channels. I call the body experience of the ally, which is essentially proprioceptive and kinesthetic, body power. Health and fitness depend upon our awareness of this body power. If you store this sense of energy in your body, it can perform incredibly.

People who have body power seem amazing to us. They have immense vitality and energy. Have you ever stored your energy instead of dissipating it? Storing power means noticing body wisdom, feelings, and the direction of energy when they are present, using and finding secondary processes when they happen. It means noticing unpredictable, subtle body feelings and following them with the second attention instead of throwing them away; and it means getting up when you are awake and lying down when you are tired.

If you neglect the body's signals, however, then you dissipate power, or negate it, so to speak, and you will be fat and old in no time.[3] You manipulate and use energy that does not belong to you and force yourself to do things against your nature.

To store power, you need to notice signals and feel when you are on track in your dreamingbody. The more you cultivate this relationship, the more congruent you are in what you do. Slowly, in time, your body will begin to feel like a dreamingbody, and you will find yourself capable of doing unpredictable things and tasks, of having more energy than you would ever have expected.

As the apprenticeship continues, don Juan advises Castaneda to trust and to let out what he calls personal power so that it can merge with what he calls the power of the night. He tells the apprentice to abandon himself to the power of the night, or he will never be free in his body. The darkness, he says, is a problem only because Castaneda relies on his normal senses and not on his "gait of power," the same power used to find his power spot.[4] The gait of power is a matter of feeling and movement. It is authentic movement and is not easy to verbalize.

Therefore, I must rely on your experiments with body feelings and recommend the following. Literally close your eyes and let your body impulses move you about. Try not to organize movement; just let it happen. If you abandon your-self to your body, you move in the right direction, that is, toward personal growth. If you do not do this, your body or ally may develop symptoms that you will be forced to follow. If you follow your body, it is an ally; otherwise, you experi-ence it as your opponent in need of healing. A shamanic view of dreambodywork is that following your body is like follow-ing the lost parts of your soul.

I have often been amazed by the movement processes of people suffering from chronic movement disorders such as Parkinson's disease or multiple sclerosis. These diseases con-tain a lot of body power. I remember one woman in particular who was suffering from multiple sclerosis. Her feet thumped uncontrollably and painfully on the floor as she tried to walk around. When Amy and I helped her exaggerate her move-ment, assuming it was part of her gait of power, she banged on the floor and began to curse a friend who had been bothering her. The more she kicked, the better she felt, and, of all things, the better she could walk. The ally in her body was trying to encourage her to be angry, using her disease to express itself. In a way, when she abandoned herself to her body, it showed her the right direction.

Body experiences are not haphazard. They are meaning-ful. The more troublesome they are, the more they seem to be potential allies. But most people sense their bodies only when they are sick and they feel the body is an enemy. By shifting attention, by using your second attention, you and everyone around you could have the body as an ally.

If you follow your body, you move through the world as if you knew it like a map. Body sensations are then experienced as if they were connected to the entire gravity and electromag-netic fields of the earth, the power of the night. The dreaming-body seems then to be partly yours and partly the connection to the universe. When you are in your dreamingbody, you ex-perience its power as not belonging to any living creature.

I remember working with a man who was dying of leukemia. He had been growing gradually weaker and now was at the end of his strength. When I arrived at his house to see him for the last time, he could hardly talk, so I laid down near him on his bed. He was a medical doctor and knew the seriousness of his situation. To my surprise, after a few moments, he suddenly mumbled to me very quietly, out of a half sleep, "The energy and power in my body are not going to die but will go into my son and you." He gave me the sense that the dreamingbody is independent of the real body and continues after death, choosing where to go next.

Power, shamans say, does not belong to anyone. It gives itself away when the time is right. This man's body power wanted to share itself. Perhaps he had been thinking before his illness that his body power, his ally, belonged only to himself. What we call life is an ally itself that is shared by those closest to us.

EXERCISES

1. Work on a path barrier. If you feel impeded by something, perhaps it is clarity, the need to understand and be in control of what is happening. Or is your problem fear, terror of what you do not know? Perhaps it is power, your possession by your potential significance or insignificance. Or the sense of being old, depressed, or detached could be hindering your energy. In any case, choose the barrier closest to you and work on it.

2. Try different ways of working on your barrier. If clarity is your barrier, use that clarity consciously. Study and plan where you are headed as much as you can. Take clarity with you on your trip; use control during times of abandon.

If your barrier is fear, focus on the thing that makes you afraid. Become the way you imagine this fearful thing to be. If your barrier is power, try telling a story about your importance or unimportance; then believe or debate with this story. Use power to change yourself instead of others.

If your barrier is old age, greet it, let it go, and die. If you were dead and freed from detachment and depression, what would you do next? Now do it.

3. Connect with your allies. Remember a wise human figure from a dream, or imagine such an inner figure now, a figure with wisdom. Take a moment and speak to this figure, and make a note of the conversation. Alternatively, remember a friendly animal you have seen in a dream, or imagine such an animal. Can you feel this animal? What is it implying?

Feel and scan your body slowly. Where do you sense your body's power, wisdom, or ally? What does it feel like there? What image fits that body area? This image is a body ally.

If you now have or ever have had body symptoms in this area, imagine your ally within these symptoms. Feel any changes in your body that occur when you identify with the ally.

Imagine that you are your ally, and give your ordinary self a message.

Finally, experiment with feeling and seeing your body wisdom all the time, not just during this experiment. If your personal history hinders this experiment, ask your ally to remove your sense of self-importance.

CHAPTER 8

THE ALLY'S SECRET

The body contains many secrets, and connection to it increases your vitality and sense of presence. Moreover, body awareness is a basic element of living in the moment. Shamans have a lot of names for body powers, such as "luminous fibers," the "will," "magic," "healing hands," and "journeying to other worlds." The exact location of body wisdom is a personal matter. You can perceive the environment with your ordinary eyes, ears, and sense of touch or with other senses of your dreamingbody. Shamans experience this dream and body phenomenon as part of the environment. Sometimes it appears as a force in the belly or as fibers that attach themselves to the world. Sometimes your dreamingbody makes you notice it as if it were an aspect of the world itself impinging upon you. Normally, you occupy or use only two or three sensory channels consciously: seeing, hearing, and perhaps smelling. But you can develop your capacity to feel as well. Then you may develop an authentic movement awareness and connect to others directly through your body's intent. I have met people who can sense the world through their back, their neck, or the center of their forehead as well as through their stomach.

To your ordinary mind, the body's acts seem haphazard. The body seems tired, awake, nervous, aroused, sick, or excited at unpredictable and awkward moments. According to many schools of medicine, the body is sick, wrong, and in need of correction when symptoms appear. These schools teach you to relax, to let go of or repress tensions and other physical events that you cannot understand.

While these schools of thought are important to understand, the dreambody message is different. It is nonpathological. From this inner viewpoint, your body is potentially wise; it perceives the world directly and has a will or intent. This intent attaches itself to events according to the significance they have for your overall growth and for the world at a given moment. The same energy that seems to oppose you in the form of an illness can unveil itself as an intent, a power with a purpose different from your consciousness. We have been able to prove this experience worldwide. But you need no outer proof, because everyone knows how the body's sudden reactions can save you and others from life-taking accidents.

Unless you know, test, and develop this ally, however, you cannot always use the body's power when you wish. If social circumstances prevent you from following the movements of your dreamingbody because such unusual movements may upset others, you can always use other channels, such as vision. You can switch back and forth between the feeling of the dreamingbody and a visualization of this feeling to find and follow the body's wisdom. Instead of doing something in movement, you can express somatic information visually or verbally.

I remember an embarrassing time years ago, when I was first beginning my practice, when I had an inexplicable urge to touch one of my clients. I had felt uneasy for several hours before I allowed myself to admit that my left hand felt compelled to touch my client's chest. I did not feel physically attracted to the woman; the impulse to touch was not sexual but was closer to the yearning for discovery. If the desire had been to touch her hand, there would not have been a problem. But her chest? Naturally, I didn't want to follow this impulse and wondered what the reasons were behind it.

I thought about it and tried to repress the urge and put it out of my mind. After a while, however, I could no longer repress my dreamingbody, and I told my client about the impulse.

She said that she trusted me and asked where my hand would go. Without knowing why, I told her where on her left breast I would touch her. She was open to experimenting, and I asked her to put her own hand there. To her surprise, she felt a lump, which she had not known was there. A subsequent biopsy proved that the tumor was malignant. She had the lump removed and made a complete recovery.

My dreamingbody was helpful to her in this instance. But it may not have been as helpful if I had not tested it, doubted it, and at first repressed it. The ally has a truth, but this can only reveal itself completely through your wrestling with it, making it as useful as possible.

The Last Dance

Thus the ally can appear in visions, body experiences, the environment, or relationships. In native traditions, body powers even withstand death. Following several native North American traditions, after a long and complete life, the warrior allows his body energy, memories, and experiences stored in the skeletal muscles to express themselves for the last time while death stands by as a witness. This "last dance," as don Juan calls it, recalls the struggles and stories of the warrior's life.

The last dance is the dreamingbody set free to express itself. In work with dying people, I have seen how the final processes of life occur in altered states of consciousness. During the last hours of life, people transcend the idea of death and perform unbelievable acts. They put off death while deeper and more important events arise.

Sogyal Rinpoche, in his *The Tibetan Book of Living and Dying*, shows that a central part of Tibetan spirituality is focused upon remaining aware during the altered states surrounding death experiences. This book is especially interesting to me. When I first encouraged people to use their awareness and follow their body impulses near death, many thought comatose people were more or less dead or not present. Western thought so far has made death only as painless as possible, not as awesome as possible. Shamans, however, follow their breathing, their coughing, even the fluttering motions of their face or limbs—their dreamingbody, or last dance. I related in chapter 7 the case of the man who was supposed to die of leukemia. The last dance I reported there put off death to such an extent that the man came back into normal life for eighteen months afterward.

But the last dance does not always happen spontaneously. Without awareness, it may not happen at all. In *Coma, Key to Awakening*, I speak about a man called Peter who was drowning from pneumonia during his last hours of life. Peter had been given an overdose of morphine so he could die painlessly and rapidly. Amy and I worked with him even as he choked, fully comatose, near death. We encouraged him to believe in himself, to go on with his coughing, whether or not it was the pneumonia he was drowning from, and to make all the noises he wanted. After several hours, he did his last dance. He spontaneously and suddenly sat up straight in the midst of the coma and stared at us with his eyes crossed. To make the story short, he came out of the comatose state, and a new consciousness arose. He talked and even sang with us for hours. As we worked further with his cough, his sputtering sounds turned into a heartwarming and ecstatic song.

It was the wee hours of the morning. The medical staff was amazed by this man's energetic activity but also disturbed because he was waking others. Through his noises, movements, and song, Peter vented all sorts of emotions—his love for the universe and for his friends and others. His dance transformed and reversed his symptoms temporarily. His throat cleared, and even his kidneys began to work again as death waited while he completed his final dance.

Death had to stand aside and witness this incredible human being. As his courageous wife stood by his side, his real body was dying, but he had climbed into his dreamingbody and was living and experiencing inner stories, feelings, and myths. His dreamingbody was living as never before, and, just before he died, he told us in a sober state that he had found the key to life.

The last dance is more awesome than can be described for those who have not experienced it. But the dreamingbody has incredible powers and intent; it wants to be complete and live as the universe lives. In my experience, this last dance may not occur without assistance, however, just as the Indian's last dance may no longer occur without the right sort of tribal shamanistic environment.

Battle with the Giver of Secrets

The dreamingbody is an ally that does not always give its message or power without a courageous encounter. Shamans find the ally's secrets during vision quests in lonely, abandoned places in nature or in other-worldly visions. This means that you can find the ally in the wilderness, in inaccessible and remote spots, or in deeply unconscious and secondary processes in your life.

You can also gain access to the ally by meditating, taking drugs, overeating, smoking, or running long distance. Don Juan gives Castaneda drugs like the devil's weed and little smoke to help him gain access to the ally's world and to knock out Castaneda's stubborn, rational primary process.

All of these methods are dangerous, however; if you do not find the ally within them, they can become addictions. In a way, an addiction like drinking alcohol or smoking is the ally's attempt to reach your awareness. For instance, if you get drunk, you may gain access to far reaches of experience, even come close to delirium or a coma, and get out of your head to find your body ally creating poetry. But alcoholism is dangerous. That is why shamans have always suggested a warrior's trainings and community support to find what they wanted and to avoid the dangers of addictions that can eventually wreak as much havoc as healing.

Alcohol especially is an immense problem among many indigenous peoples, including shamans. In my experience with such peoples, alcohol is a symptom of trying to find dreamtime in cosmopolitan reality; it is a symptom of a loss of rootedness in wholeness and dreaming, and of the depression and pain of oppression and disenfranchisement. Drugs are a means of getting around personal history and journeying to other realms to find the missing pieces of reality. But without carefulness, drugs become a destructive ally.

It is important to battle with the ally. Don Juan recommends that, when facing the ally, you gather all your courage and grab the ally before it demolishes you, go after it before it hunts you. You must continue this chase until you connect and the struggle begins. Then you must "wrestle the spirit to the ground" and hold it there until it gives you power.[1]

The battle with the ally can occur in ordinary consciousness or in dreams. One of this book's reviewers had an immense dream about the ally's secret. In this dream, she met and battled an ally. She describes the dream as follows: "I was standing by a lake, and an unusual fish rose out of the water. I got scared because it had such a long nose. It was fat and looked like a pig with fluorescent pink-and-yellow colors, as if it had been painted. I batted it on the nose, because I was scared of it, so it would go away. It went back down, and then it came back up again and talked to me. It said, 'Your problem is that you are too rational and need to be more irrational!'"

The dream has special characteristics that belong to this woman, but the bat on the nose was her battle with the ally. She was worried at the time of the dream about her worldly responsibilities. When she played with the colorful fish-pig in her imagination, it complained and said that it did not want to work. It wanted her to be a pig, make a mess, and relax.

The pig within this woman did not talk until she battled with it in her dream. It is important that she first resisted or hit the fish; she did not just accept it or become possessed by it. That would have meant that she would just be a pig, overeat, or become messy. After she pushed it back into the water, the ally came out a second time with its secret, the real message: Be more irrational. The power coming from the fish was the encouragement to examine the unknown in life.

Tezcatlipoca

Don Juan's description of the battle with the ally must be related to ancient mythical Aztec stories about a terrifying god, the feared Tezcatlipoca. According to the Aztec legend, the Aztecs thought that Tezcatlipoca wandered at night in the shape of a giant, wrapped in an ash-colored veil and carrying his head in his hand. When nervous people saw him, they died. But the brave man seized the giant, saying he would not let Tezcatlipoca go until sunrise. The giant begged to be released and then cursed. If the man succeeded in holding the monster until daylight, Tezcatlipoca changed his tune and offered wealth and invincible power if the man would set him free. The victorious man received four thorns as a pledge from the conquered. The brave man tore out the heart of Tezcatlipoca and took it home; but when he unwrapped the cloth in which he had folded it, he found nothing but white feathers, a thorn, ashes, or an old rag.[2] The archetypal ally Tezcatlipoca is likened to the summer sun, bringer of life. But near the equator, the sun also becomes a killer. Tezcatlipoca appears to us as a personal spirit, but the spirit belongs to the universe, just as the sun belongs both to the earth and to the cosmos.

The archetypal and most powerful ally is different from a protective figure such as Buddha, Jesus, or a dead parent; it is an impossible god of darkness. In the Aztec myth, it is portrayed as the most terrifying experience, the thing that scares you most and that is furthest from your ability to control.

According to the legend of Tezcatlipoca, you must wrestle with the ally and chase it before it chases you; that is, you need to get its secret but not become possessed by it. If the ally is the kernel of an altered state of consciousness, a message presaged in illness, irrational movements, and impulses, then wrestling the ally means processing with it to find its meaning. Wrestle with the sense of being possessed; pull the message out of fearful fantasies, out of the air and down to the ground, or you might lose precious information. Wrestle with an addiction to get its message. Struggle with physical pain until its gives its message. Ask the gods why they have created life as they have.

What is Tezcatlipoca's secret message? According to the myth, it is white feathers, a thorn, ashes, or an old rag. These gifts symbolize spiritual qualities with no immediate worldly values. The key to life is an old rag, a feather, ashes—not something to do or achieve, but a feeling about life. In the dream of the pig-fish with the long nose, the gift is the feeling that life is a crazy and irrational place and must be lived in that way.

The encounter with the ally is potentially lethal. If you have ever been terrified by a possibly dangerous illness, you know what that encounter with the ally feels like. The bottom line is death. You either get the ally's information or fear for your life. On the other hand, if you become infatuated with the ally, you get carried away by it and can become addicted to its power unleashed by a drug.

Sacrifice to the Ally

This may be why the Aztecs feared Tezcatlipoca more than any other god and offered him blood sacrifices. They believed he had the power to destroy the world if he so wished. Every year, they chose the most handsome prisoner to personify that god. The prisoner was taught to sing and play the flute, to wear flowers, and to smoke elegantly. He was richly garbed, and eight pages were assigned to wait on him. For a whole year, he was heaped with honors and pleasure. Twenty days before the date fixed for his sacrifice, he received four young women as his wives, personifications of four goddesses. Then began a series of festivals and dances. Finally, when the fatal day arrived, the young man was taken with great pomp out of the town and sacrificed on the last terrace of the temple. The priest opened the breast of the prisoner with one cut of his obsidian knife and tore out the palpitating heart, which he offered to the sun.[3]

What is the meaning of this dreadful sacrifice of the most handsome prisoner bonded to the four goddesses (ignoring for the moment the repellent sexism in this and other myths)? The story must be trying to say that you need to serve your ally god and sacrifice your worldly good looks, your success. Since Tezcatlipoca is the sun, you must first honor or consciously give to the impulse to burn, to live ecstatically. This sacrifices a part of your ordinary self and makes you a kind of criminal, because ecstasy is repressed in most societies. Once you serve your ally, old parts of you die, as new parts connected to transpersonal experience begin to live.

If you are gifted with an ally and do not go through this process consciously, the ally can kill you. Think of the musical composer Wolfgang Amadeus Mozart, for example. This great man served his musical ally genius. He wrote music but was possessed by alcohol, which finally killed him, still in his early thirties. Though no one can judge another human, I often wonder what would have happened to Mozart had he lived more with his ally and slain the good-looking, worldly part of himself, as Aztec myths suggest. Instead, he tried to live a middle-class, bourgeois life (though his alcoholism made this almost impossible). Saying no to alcohol and yes to its divine manifestation might have meant saying yes to creativity and no to his standard lifestyle.

It's easier to speak of this battle than to live it yourself, however. If you have ever felt inspired, you know some of the good feelings of being driven by a powerful ally. You also know the toll that ally takes on ordinary living and friendships.

Meetings with allies are presaged in nightmarish childhood dreams in which you barely escape the monster's clutches. Often, these early dream figures catch you, predicting the crises that will occur periodically later on in life. At every point as you continue through life, monsters seem to threaten your ability to adapt by provoking behavior that seems unacceptable. There are the crises of your school days, when the ally makes you act more complicated than your school system or parents wish. Then there are your twenties, during which you tussle with choosing a profession; the ally is always convinving you to change professions or choose one that seems unrealistic. The ally is there again in the crisis of midlife, threatening to overturn your whole life, disturbing relationships, and throwing life into apparent confusion. Finally, in old age, the demon appears again, making you irritable and impossible, reducing your tolerance for worldly pursuits, and meddling in the affairs of friends and relatives.

Again and again, the ally appears in your moods and disturbs relationships. Since your problems come from other dimensions, you never feel that you are the cause of your troubles. But others think you are. You, meanwhile, insist that they are the difficulty.

Your most ancient human task is to recover everything that makes you whole, to find your soul, to discover your demon. This means noticing where that demon is and then processing its uncanny energies. Remember the woman with multiple sclerosis I mentioned in chapter 7? If you think of the body problem as the ally, the message to this woman was to be unpredictable, to express all her feelings. Because she was courageous, she could do this. To seek the ally's secret and find the key to existence before you are driven to madness or illness takes a lot of courage.

The ally, the ghost that spooks you, is more than your personal demon. Like Tezcatlipoca, the ally is a cosmic star, a universal deity, something in the atmosphere everywhere. It is in your family, your group, and your nation. The ally is a neglected collective spirit. It is the outlaw, the shadow of your whole community, that aspect of culture that will not abide by the present system.

Thus, the demon is everyone's disorder, but also everyone's potential future renewal. It acts out an important role in the world, a role typically missing in culture; it is the mad you, the perverted you, the ecstatic you, the rebel, the suffering and wise you. From earliest childhood, you have dealt with not only your personal demon, but the world's most unacceptable psychology. The battle with your personal ally is simultaneously global work.

The gods and spirits are not only yours but everyone's. You suffer from fantasies and body problems that not only plague you, but are found in everyone's dreams about the same time. Your suffering is the mythic conflict between the spirit of the times in which you live and the unknown demon of renewal. That is why, if you are a successful warrior, your battle not only turns the demon into a helpful adviser but will relieve the atmosphere around you. As you forge your own basic nature anew, you change the world, a shaman who battles with demons to protect her community.

With each battle, you come closer to something eternal, and dropping your personal history becomes easier. The ally demands not only momentary change, but a total reappraisal of your personal identity and worldview. Your gods and goddesses demand that you accept your mythical nature and undertake feats that you think should be left to the gods.

Remember Peter, the dying man I mentioned earlier in this chapter? As he came out of his coma, he yelled, again and again, "I have found the key to life!" Amy and I never did completely understand what that key was, but the last dream he had before dying gave us a hint. In that dream, he was lost, but he found his way by following the gigantic footsteps of a mythic figure through the snow. He was following the foot-steps of his ally through the unknown, across the threshold of physical life. The ally, appearing in the gyrations of his own incredible dying body, was showing him the way to eternity.

EXERCISES

1. When you feel ready to work with the ally, consider the events in your life that have been most difficult, terrifying, baffling, or blocking.

2. Choose one such difficult accident, symptom, relationship problem, or nightmare.

3. Study the threat. Feel its nature. Focus upon it. What does it feel like to be its victim?

4. Now prepare for a switch. Experiment with leaving your old victim identity behind for a moment and stepping outside the problem. When you are ready, experiment with becoming the creator of your problem. If it was an accident, feel or imagine a powerful force or ally that could have created it. If it is a symptom, feel or imagine the nature of a spirit that created the symptom, whose power you have been feeling, and then imagine being that spirit. Feel the symptom maker, and make a picture of it. Try creating a human face. If your problem is a relationship difficulty, imagine or feel some being that could make this relationship so difficult. Paint or draw this spirit; play it or ask a friend to play it for you.

5. When you are ready, confront the spirit. Get its message. Wrestle with the ally by questioning it as you play it. Feel its message, and find out what aspect of yourself, if any, it opposes in your personal life. Can you change in some small way? Can you sacrifice or transform your personal life to incorporate the power of this demon so that it is your ally? How could the ally eventually enrich the culture in which you are presently living?

6. Feel the energy of the ally, and imagine employing it usefully in a worldly task right away.

7. Take some time to get ready to sing and dance. Finally, get the ally to dance and sing. Move with its energy, getting it to make sounds in accordance with your movements. Get it to sing a song with words. Don't forget to record its song. After all, if you have gotten this far, you have wrestled the ally to the ground and found its secret.

CHAPTER 9

THE DOUBLE

Gradual changes in your identity take place as you work on yourself patiently for years. You get to know your moods; your problems transmute as their original apocalyptic visage takes on a more human form. During this time, you become more creative and live closer to your body energy and dreams. It almost seems as if your ally has disappeared, or at least it shows up in your dreams in less dramatic forms. Sometimes it even bears resemblance to you.

This transformation of you into the ally and the ally into you is a product of increasing congruity and wholeness, foreshadowed in the Aztec myth of

Tezcatlipoca. The name Tezcatlipoca means "smoking mirror." The ally's mirrorlike aspect is that he reflects the face that fights him. Thus, the ally is the forerunner of the double—the picture of your eternal, whole self; the dreamingbody with your face.

Now you can see why hunting and warriorship play such prime roles in the works of many modern authors on shamanism. The central focus on warriorship today is not due to history, because shamans and indigenous cultures did not focus intensely upon this aspect of spiritual life. The term "warrior" does not even appear in the index of *Shamanism*, Eliade's seminal work!

The momentary emphasis upon warriorship is connected more to the period you are living in than to ancient times. As you move toward a new century, you are confronted with greater diversity than your tribal relatives had to deal with in their ethnic groups. You no longer live in an ethnically homogeneous tribe. Your present culture is more diverse than anyone would ever have guessed possible. You are faced with the approach of a global village without having learned how to get along with one another. We seem unable to avoid racism, poverty, homophobia, harming the environment, crime, and other issues. No one can repress diversity issues. Hence, your unconscious fascination with war and also with warriorship.

But the outer dimension of your predicament is internal as well. Racism, for example, can only arise in an individual who has cut himself off from the color or nature of others within himself. White people of European ancestry need to affirm the nature of all those whom they colonized. People of the Americas are one-sided without recognizing the Native American spirit in themselves; Australians are like rootless trees without connection to aboriginal life. You are inadvertently racist if you only accept one side of yourself. You can try to ban others from your concept of the world, but you won't succeed this way with your own soul. Just think of it: Australians only recently gave aboriginal people the right to vote. And many so-called modern people still think shaman-ism and indigenous groups are savage. These prejudices create splits, tensions, and fascinations in war and warriorship.

As you grow wiser, you find yourself becoming more concerned with people whom you have repressed. New con-flicts may arise within you because of the parts of life you have repressed. You need and needed warriorship, but once you have met your ally, you come together, and it seems as if warriorship were only a phase of life for you. Perhaps with-out ever having noticed this phase, you freed yourself and picked up parts of yourself that you were not ready to admit earlier in your life.

From the present vantage point, the battle with the ally has been a battle with yourself and with a part of your culture that has been repressed. Now, as your fascination with war abates, you wonder why everyone else seems to be so pos-sessed with power issues.

As your innerwork, discipline, courage, and steadfast-ness transform into a new work, you find yourself less at war and more at harmony with the inner world that you reflect. In fact, before you know it, you begin to develop a double, as your outer appearance begins to match your inner one.

Modern literature on consciousness has not paid suffi-cient attention to the study of the double, and so it is a plea-sure to begin here with the double's empirical nature and the stories of the shaman guru don Genaro.

The Double and Double Signals

Have you ever wondered why you may dream of an ani-mal or weird situation after having been upset by some inter-action at work or with a friend? A shaman's view of this dreaming process would be that neither you nor your friends are themselves. You are all animals or weird-looking beings.

Likewise, when don Juan helps Castaneda call up images of his friends through the use of fantasy, all of Castaneda's friends appear as symbols, such as mushrooms, tigers, or other animals. Don Juan says that these figures represent the friends' allies.

In other words, fantasies and dreams of your friends are images of their essential but unintegrated nature. You are going into dreaming dimensions to actually see what was missing from or happening in reality. You just did not know it. Thus, your dreaming sees your friends' unconscious, their secondary processes, in the symbols or dreamlike figures that govern their actions.

In a way, you are always dreaming about the hidden powers behind everyday life, behind surface reality. Dreams depict disavowed aspects of the world. In ordinary reality, you do not focus on these aspects—rejected selves and unrepresented, hidden aspects of the environment.

However, you may have a friend who is her real self in everyday life. She actually behaves the way she is and thus appears as herself in your dreams. Castaneda, for example, is shocked to discover that one of his shaman mentors does not appear as a symbol in his fantasies. Genaro appears to Castaneda as Genaro himself. Castaneda is so stunned that don Juan tries to calm him down by explaining: Genaro is now his "twin." There is no possible way to decide whether he is real or not, yet Genaro's double, according to don Juan, is just as real as the man himself. Genaro's double, in fact, *is* the self, and this explanation should be sufficient.[1]

This explanation would suffice if you were a practicing and enlightened Taoist. But you probably identify yourself with the time, space, physical body, and doings of Western culture. When the shaman explains that Genaro is neither real nor unreal, neither a dream nor reality, neither dead nor alive, he means that the sorcerer identifies himself as much with the spirit that moves him as he does with the world. There is no longer a difference between the two. He is at once real, unreal, and neither.

If someone is his total self, you see him as himself in your fantasies and visions. That is why Genaro in dreamland looks as he would on the street: He is whole. How did Genaro get to be this way? He could just be congruent. Or he might have been in therapy for years. Or other shamans may have journeyed into forgotten realms to find split-off parts of his soul. Perhaps he simply inherited the shamanic spirit and no longer acts one way while feeling another.

In terms of processwork, you normally identify with primary processes and disavow secondary ones. You develop edges against your secondary experiences. If you were hurt as a child, parts of your childlike nature are split off and appear only in dreams. If you were afraid to be handsome or beautiful when you were a teenager, or if no one wanted to dance with you, the teenager may have left your conscious mind and gone into another world. You may have put all of your animal nature away if the people who brought you up were afraid of their own instincts.

In any case, you end up split into parts. These parts are in the underworld or the celestial realms, as shamans have discovered. Today we also know that they are present but disavowed parts of the moment. They appear in your body signals, even if you are not conscious of them and if others cannot make sense of your double signals, that is, the behavior with which you do not identify.

For example, if your childhood was difficult, you will repress your childlike instinct and whine and complain instead of playing. If you repress these signals, your friends become confused and dream about these signals as childlike figures to which you feel unconnected. Hence, you can appear in others' dreams as a baby, a fairy, a monster, a businessman, or a guru, depending upon what you disavow at a given moment.

Your dreams and body signals give you a chance to find yourself again. Dreams display parts of the world that you can learn to recognize inside yourself and also in your friends. Consider the possibility that your experiences, fantasies, dreams, and body sensations, all aspects of the dreamingbody, are specific to a given environment and moment in time. In this way, awareness means not only personal innerwork but outerwork as well. Awareness means waking up to the nature of the world around you.

An example of how this may work comes to mind. Amy and I decided to experiment with being our whole selves with a mutual friend, Rachel. We each took the task of recognizing our own double signals and then living them, of living our dreamingbody.

As we began, Rachel found herself flirting. She used her second attention on herself and focused on signals that seemed like flirting to her. She experimented, flirted, and made eyes at me. Meanwhile, Amy, who was studying her own signals, found her shoulders moving. She too used her second attention, held these movements in her consciousness, and began to allow them to unfold. She followed her arms, which were trying to flap, and suddenly she became a wild bird. Amy screeched at Rachel for flirting, making us all laugh uncontrollably. We were people, but we could just as well have been three birds working out a relationship conflict.

We recovered from our laughter, and I tried to find out what was happening with me. I noticed that I was trying to act as if nothing disturbed me. Then I found myself pulling my head in and realized that the two women had frightened me. Getting into my double, I ran away from them both, screaming for safety from their powers. Again, we all broke into laughter.

When I asked myself what I was running from, I realized that it was not only their power but my own neediness. I felt undeserving of all their attention and was afraid to ask for it. I took courage and asked for help. I had problems of my own and asked them to help me with them. The two women did the same sometime afterward. By getting into our double signals, we were congruent for that moment. We were living our doubles.

Fields and Projections

You may ask if you are just dreaming or projecting your own inner images onto your friends when you dream of them.

The answer to this is yes, a projection occurs every time something inside of you finds an outer object to hang itself upon. But, whereas projection is an idea coming mainly from individual psychology, the double is a field concept. If a certain image is in the field around you, then you find it in your dreams, and others may dream or experience it as well. Field concepts are shared experiences, so to speak. They are products of your personal psychology and of the psychology of others around you, but they are more than that. They belong to the entire field.

Your double can be located in a certain space and time, but from the outside, it may seem parapsychological. Others may see you anywhere on earth. If shamans knew physics, they might say that you were yourself and yet also a part of a universal quantum field.

The simplest way to develop a double is through your dreaming. In your dreaming world, you can put the parts of yourself together. In process terms, you arrive at the double by becoming aware of secondary processes, noticing dreamlike experiences during waking life, and sensing and living the energy of impulses and figures until they become you. Don't wait until the night to dream; dream now, and dream constantly. This is a matter of awareness in feeling, moving, seeing, hearing, and relating.

Notice how you are trying to act; then notice if anything else is happening, and if it is, step into it. The big problem is stepping out of your old identity and into the dreaming process—stopping the world, so to speak. As you develop awareness of your feelings, let your body sensations direct your behavior. This is developing the double through dreaming.

The less connected you are to yourself, the more you make teachers and gurus out of people who are connected to themselves. You describe them as wise, terrifying, loving, and powerful. When you experience such body powers yourself, you tend to think of them afterward as unusual trips. But while you are living your dreamingbody, you do not feel awesome, terrifying, or powerful. You just feel well, present, and at home.

The double becomes real for you when you live your secondary processes and get around doubts and hesitations. Take responsibility, and live what you perceive and experience, regardless of what others might think.

Stepping Out of Time

You may appear to step out of time and even seem to appear in two places at once. Don Juan explains to Castaneda that a warrior who is fluid does not focus on ordinary time, since he does not experience himself as an object. The warrior only notices afterward that he has been in two places at once. This has been only "bookkeeping"; it has not influenced him while he was acting fluidly.

Don Juan says that, for the warrior like Genaro, there is only one process. Only the outsider thinks the warrior is in the midst of two different episodes. The warrior notices only afterward that he has had two separate experiences, "because the glue of the description of time is no longer binding."

This is a highly differentiated understanding of perception and sounds more like modern psychology than ancient shamanism. Or perhaps we are beginning now to integrate the worlds. In any case, a parapsychological event may be seen from two viewpoints. Magical events can be experienced in at least two ways: by the outside observer and by the shaman living them.

As an outsider, you live in ordinary time and space, in a given social or community context. You behave like everyone else. Your intention and identity belong to that time and area. When you look at secondary processes, since you do not participate in their flow, they appear symbolic, strange, and erratic. You see your own acts as events outside the rules of normal behavior; they break social codes and even the laws of time and space. As an outsider you think that you are either a warrior who has a physical body located in a given place at a certain time, or you are a projection or a figment of the imagination.

Since you act as if you only see "real" bodies, you think that you must be a spirit who can step out of your body and be in two places at one time. That is why Castaneda thinks he sees Genaro in one place when Genaro is in another. He assumes that Genaro must have developed a double. If Castaneda were with Genaro, inside the experience—if he could participate and step into the river of dreams—he would realize that Genaro is simply real wherever he is experienced.

If you are in your dreamingbody, then everything is real, and you feel life is as it should be. If, however, you are in a normal state of consciousness, identified with your primary process and the doings of the everyday world, then you are shocked and amazed when some of your dreams seem real, and you call them synchronicities, or doubles. Likewise, you think others who are congruent are also magicians.

In one story in *Tales of Power*, don Juan and Castaneda try to escape from a friend of Castaneda's who wants to meet don Juan. Outside a modern office building, don Juan gives Castaneda a shove between his shoulders and sends him reeling through the office, through space and time. The shove disorients Castaneda to such a degree that he travels backward in time to a marketplace on the previous Saturday and wanders through scenes that had happened then. He actually witnesses events that took place a week earlier in a place he had never been.

Though improbable, going backward in time is possible, according to the rules of physics. Antimatter is the same as ordinary matter, but it is short-lived. Richard Feynman, a Nobel Prize–winning physicist, developed a theory of antimatter that reminds me of don Juan's double. Feynman had two stories of what happened to an electron in a field: the insider's and the outsider's stories.

Feynman's outsider theory states that when an electron enters a magnetic field, new parts of matter are temporarily created. A new electron and its antimatter double, a positron, appear. Next, all three particles—the old electron, together with the electron-positron couple—travel forward in time together until the positron, or double, eventually annihilates the original, old electron within the field. Meanwhile, the second, new electron continues on outside the magnetic field. No one notices, of course, that this electron is any different from the original one. These creations and annihilations are something like a story of being killed by your double and then being reincarnated.

Feynman used a second story to also explain what happened to the original electron, a story without extra creations or annihilations. He used an insider's viewpoint. He said that the first electron was fluid. Instead of getting annihilated by its ally, it could become a fluid warrior, notice trouble coming, and change. It could become its own double and travel backward in time. From this perspective, you don't need concepts like matter and antimatter, but must consider that an electron in a magnetic field can go backward in time and then forward again. The electron becomes temporarily paranormal, that is, free of time and space.

Thus, acts like feeling yourself going backward in time are equivalent to living like antimatter in the quantum mechanical world. You either bump into your ally or step out of time and become eternal. In ordinary life, you might appear to others as if you were part of a mysterious, parapsychological event. If you have a double and are a warrior following your dreamingbody, such stories are normal.

Living the dreamingbody is simple: You do it spontaneously if you have the courage to follow what you feel and improvise life as it comes. Yet for the ordinary observer who does not sense the dreamingbody, and who is therefore on the outside, anything that does not correspond to consensus reality is an awesome, incomprehensible sorcerer's act.

The chance to experiment with the double and step out of time and space, out of your primary processes, presents itself any time you begin to feel unusual or any time you are caught in the midst of a situation that excites you. Loaded, tense, or complex situations split you into parts.

Consider, for example, walking at night along a dark forest path or speaking in front of a large group of people. These activities separate you into parts. One part identifies with your shy or scared self, and another is connected to imagined malevolent, evil forces in the forest or critical people in the group. Naturally, you disidentify and disavow the malevolent, powerful side of yourself. A shaman, however, applies her second attention to this force to find out more about it.

In any case, you suddenly find yourself being two things at once: the victim and the critical, menacing figure. While the average you becomes split, disavowing the evil forces and the dreams and double signals about them, the aware you becomes both parts, first one and then the other. As a shaman, you let the world provoke or direct you. You remain your normal self, enjoying the evening walk until your fear comes up. Then you notice this fear, apply your second attention, perceive the monster, and behave unpredictably. You might become the powerful monster and start growling instead of splitting off the monster. Or you might start running for your life, letting your body take you wherever it wants to go. An outside observer would notice that you are breaking the rules of normal behavior and think you are hilarious, mad, or parapsychological.

I once heard a story about a meeting of the American Humanistic Psychology Association. Abe Maslow was conducting the meeting. Suddenly Fritz Perls was seen crawling under the table at which Maslow was sitting. "Papa, be nice to me, please be nice," Perls whimpered from the floor, while pulling on the leg of Maslow's trousers. Perls was living his double, following the will of his dreamingbody. Yet his little child role must also have been a part of the group atmosphere that was not represented.

Large group scenes create complex fields. This may be why you tend to avoid large groups, for they bring up aspects of yourself that you want to avoid.

Dying people seem to automatically get into their dreamingbodies and travel through time and space. I was able to substantiate this with a Swiss client who told me several days before he died, while we were sitting together in Zurich in the 1970s, that he was in Hamburg at a stoplight on a certain street where there was a traffic jam. I called a friend I knew in Hamburg and discovered that there was a real traffic jam on that otherwise quiet street at that moment. From the outsider's viewpoint, the dying man was in Hamburg and also in Zurich. He was in two places at the same time. From his viewpoint, he was living in his dreamingbody. At one moment he was with me, and at another he was in Hamburg.

Secondary processes, like dreams, may be linked to the entire world. Your personal life is not only personal. From the outsider's viewpoint, you suffer from dreams, body problems, neuroses, and relationship and world problems. But from the insider's viewpoint, you are everywhere at once and have the chance to step out of space and time and be anywhere, at any time.

The ordinary way you live is probably on a path without much heart. It mercilessly carries you about as a piece of lifeless matter. You kick yourself about as well, pushing yourself unconsciously, acting as if you determine your own fate. The path of heart, however, is illuminated by the warrior's viewpoint. When something new comes up, the warrior intensifies it, tightens himself, and steps out of his prescribed venue to avoid time and perhaps even death.

Dreaming the Self

Don Juan calls the act of developing a double stopping the world, stepping out of the identity you have. He says that your ordinary self dreams the double. However, once you have learned to dream the double, things reverse, and you realize that, actually, the double dreams the self. You yourself are a dream, because the double is dreaming you, just as you normally think you have dreamed it.[2]

You normally identify yourself with the everyday self, your primary process, because your personal history and identity are important to you. But the more you become aware of secondary processes, the more it becomes possible to stop your normal identity. In the moment you do that, your dreamingbody becomes the base reality, which seems to dream up your ordinary world in order to realize itself.

You know that your dreamingbody, or your double, really creates what you experience as ordinary life, trouble, and body symptoms, because you dream up problems when you get bored. You have no other way to announce who you are except to disturb yourself and limit yourself with ordinary life.

In his autobiography, Jung tells of an encounter he had with the double just before his death.

> I had dreamed once before of the problem of the self (i.e., double) and the ego. In that earlier dream I was on a hiking trip. I was walking along a little road through a hilly landscape; the sun was shining and I had a wide view in all directions. Then I came to a small wayside chapel. The door was ajar, and I went in. To my surprise there was no image of the Virgin on the altar, and no crucifix either, but only a wonderful flower arrangement. But then I saw that on the floor in front of the altar, facing me, sat a yogi—in lotus posture, in deep meditation. When I looked at him more closely, I realized that he had my face. I started in profound fright, and awoke with the thought: "Aha, so he is the one who is meditating me. He has a dream, and I am it." I knew that when he awakened, I would no longer be."[3]

Jung explains that his dream represents "his unconscious as the generator of the empirical personality." He says that this dream showed a reversal of reality. Rather than see life from the viewpoint of the normal identity, the ego, this dream shows that the ego is the dream of the unconscious. He says, "Our unconscious existence is the real one and our conscious world a kind of illusion, an apparent reality constructed for a specific purpose, like a dream which seems a reality as long as we are in it. . . . Unconscious wholeness therefore seems to me the true spiritus rector of all biological and psychic events."[4]

The spiritus rector, the guiding spirit of life, is what you are when you identify and step into a secondary process. Then you are your double, the maker of dreams, body life, and uncontrollable world events. Jung's spiritus rector, your dreamingbody, and the shaman's double dreamed up the world we all live in.

EXERCISES

1. Close your eyes and imagine that you are dreaming about your friends, one after another. Who are these friends? Which ones are themselves? Which are animals, trees, children, or dragons?

Recommend to your friends that they experiment with acting like the animals or other images in your dreams and fantasies. After the experiment, ask them how close your images are to aspects of themselves that they have not taken seriously. Discuss with them how your imagination of them is a shared altered state of consciousness that you also have within you.

2. Develop your double. Ask a friend to sit with you and to close her eyes and dream or imagine who you really are. Now, as an experiment, try to become the person in your friend's imagination. Discuss afterward how close her vision comes to your reality. How close is her vision to what is needed in the relationship between you?

3. Develop your double in public. What sorts of outer situations or fields upset you or get you into emotional trouble? Re-create the outer scene in your imagination or with some friends. Now notice how you are trying to behave, and also notice which feelings you are rejecting. Instead of letting these feelings make you incongruent, let the rejected feelings move you to speak, dance, or sing. Get into your dreamingbody, and become a role in that field. Is this role needed in some way by everyone? Is it a missing spirit? Now set this up and practice it the next time you are in public.

CHAPTER 10

THE PATH
OF HEART

The dreamingbody begins to manifest itself in everyday life with training in awareness, picking up unusual movements, and feeling strange. In time, awareness skills work almost automatically. You find yourself more lucid and awake even while you are engaged in the most mundane of activities, such as sleeping, shopping, talking with friends, working, and so on.

But then something unexpected happens. As you become more lucid, you may find yourself forgetting those awareness skills that you worked so hard to learn. You now have times when you are simply wakeful. Something fogs out the memory of how you arrived at the present place of awareness.

This development is typical in many psychological and spiritual traditions.

Zen succinctly explains this development: Before Zen, a mountain is a mountain; during Zen, a mountain is no longer a mountain; and after Zen, a mountain is a mountain again. In other words, before you begin your awareness training, life is normal—either full of trouble or just fine. Suddenly, you are aware of dream figures and ghosts, of unconscious and conscious parts, of your secondary and primary processes. Everything contains hidden messages and meanings. The world is full of parts, complexes, shame, repression, childhood pain, allies, signals, and abuse. You must be a warrior to survive. You discipline yourself and lead a tight life.

Finally, after Zen, there are no longer any hidden meanings; the world is itself again. At this stage, there seems at times to be nothing to think about. The drive to understand the world as composed of things and parts—soul and body—diminishes. You forget about being a hunter, a warrior, and even that incredible ally. Instead, you experience only periods of ongoing awareness. You learn through your feelings and intuitions to be more congruent. You go back and forth between the worlds without calling them separate. You even wonder why others speak of separate realities, of individual and environment, of human being and nature, of conscious and unconscious. Sometimes you even think that others are wrong and that you have seen the light.

But you must be careful. The next step in the Zen story should read, "and the mountain crumbled and had to be re-created again." If you are not going to be wrecked by the barrier of old age, the training has to start all over again. It is easy to see how lucky an apprentice is to have found a master, but you should also remember that the master is lucky to be troubled by the stubborn beginner. Left to himself, a good teacher never seems to have the energy to reveal the crucial details of his discoveries, the necessary overview and compassion that help others. The apprentice forces the teacher to begin again.

I love to think of Lao Tsu, the legendary author of the *Tao Te Ching*, that ancient and core classic text of Taoism. According to legend, a town's gatekeeper stopped Lao Tsu as he was leaving the city in advanced old age and begged the ancient master to write down his wisdom. Without the struggle between the gatekeeper and the Taoist master, we would not have the teachings of the *Tao Te Ching* today.

Old age is a barrier unless you are a curious and stubborn beginner who constantly wonders about fundamental questions and the overall meaning of life. Don't you often ask yourself, What is the meaning of life? What is this world all about? Though there are no general answers, still there are guidelines, depending upon the school of psychology that interests you, the spiritual tradition, race, and religion.

One answer from the world of the shaman is that life is about ecstatic journeys into other dimensions. It is not only about solving problems or finding lost souls out there. That is good enough. But it is really more. For a shaman, life itself is an ecstatic journey, full of trance, ascent to celestial realms, and battles with the underworld. Life is about the adventure of altered states. At the same time, it is the greatest detective mystery there is.

Mirroring many Native American traditions, don Juan answers questions about what life is all about by the "path of heart." As his teachings draw to a close in *A Separate Reality,* don Juan drops the jargon and paraphernalia of warriorship and centers upon shamanism's bare essentials, the feelings or metaskills behind the work and not just the tools of shamanism. He advises Castaneda that, upon returning to his everyday life, he will be confronted by important problems and will no longer be able to live as he previously has lived. A warrior needs an overview. He needs much more than skill; he needs wisdom to continue living and dealing with the problems of everyday life.

Don Juan recommends finding and following the path of heart. Any process you follow is just one of many possible paths. Therefore, you must remember that "a path is only a path." If the path you are on feels wrong, then you should feel free to drop it. Every path is relative, and knowing whether to stay on or to leave your path requires clarity and self-knowledge. Your heart will tell you when it is time to leave a path and when it is time to stay on it.[1]

The Old Path

Sometimes you continue with old paths, even when your heart tells you not to. You may be staying on a path because it is the only one you know. Out of fear, you dare not think of yourself as anything but a daughter, son, partner, father, mother, executive, housewife, or student. Fears of new roles, financial insecurity, and even closed-mindedness to new experiences keep you from significantly changing and living your dreamingbody in the world. You feel obliged both to yourself and to others to maintain the personal history you have created. Personal history is a prison that you seem to have created for yourself.

Another drive that keeps you stubbornly on a path is ambition. You may be convinced that the path you have chosen will not succeed, yet you feel it must. Thus you spend most of your time trying to achieve success on the path even when the effort is agonizing. In addition, you stay on these paths not only because of pride and hope for success, but because you believe that you alone must create success, even when your heart tells you that something feels wrong. You know that life is trying to redirect you, but you cannot listen.

You may also stay on your chosen path because you feel tired and finished. You have been through so much already that changing paths at this point seems impossible. Together with depression, exhaustion convinces you that nothing matters, that the world situation is hopeless and will never change.

Discipline

Western psychologically oriented teachers say that you need a strong ego to make important decisions about your

ARNOLD MINDELL

life The shamans say that you need a disciplined life to determine whether a path is right or not. There is a crucial difference between Western and Eastern teachings, between what you might call modern European and aboriginal or spiritual thinking.

Psychological and spiritual systems require either an ego director, which determines what should happen, or a disciplined awareness, which notices what is happening. Systems based upon the development of ego consciousness stress stability and individuation. Self-knowledge is the core. Indigenous systems stress becoming everything or worshiping nature and finding a path with heart.

Each system has a part of the truth. The right tradition is the one you believe in at any given moment. When you are interested in the future of the world, however, you find yourself searching for paths with heart. They make you keep a watchful eye on your own sustainable and available energy and upon relationships to others. Indigenous heartful systems include community and environment. The ego system informs you more about the nature of specific parts of yourself. When you need answers about your individual nature, you find yourself with therapists, who speak of unknown parts. When you have questions about life as a whole, the environment and path of heart are the teachers.

To find the path of heart—to follow the stream of nature—you need more disciplined awareness than self-knowledge. For the path of heart is simply the path that is "easy"; it is the ancient Tao, but no one can follow this Tao without awareness of what is happening. In those moments in which you use your second attention, feel your dreaming-body, and find the Tao, you know that you are on track, because, whether you are working hard or not, you feel like you are not using any energy. Everything happens of its own accord, and you seem to be riding a wave on the path of least resistance. Though you may be in the midst of a whirlwind, still it is the path of least action, the path sometimes referred to in Taoism as "not doing," or "wu wei."

Courage

You also need courage in order to find the path, because when you change, those around you may be affronted. They feel your changes hurt them, and then they may seek revenge. Since friends and colleagues have been a part of the old path, some may not support your changes.

Thus, to have heart, you need courage to detach from other's opinions. With courage and discipline, you notice that you are a secondary process for the whole community. It is not you alone who wants to change, but a cultural path that wants to change. Your changes may therefore somehow be right for everyone else.

Heart is different from sentimentality. Sentimentality attaches you to the way things are and prevents you from changing when the time comes. If you are sentimental, you listen too long to the fears and complaints of others. Or perhaps the others are a part of you that resists change. In any case, you wait, taking time to grow and gain detachment. One day you realize that your choice to leave a path and follow the one with heart affronts others because you are their nagual, their dreamlike fate.

For the teenager who must fight her parents, the parent who becomes a teenager in love, the teacher who leaves his students, or the group member who revolts, change creates momentary suffering. Hence, you need an inner discipline and courage to keep your mind on eternity while caring for the pain of the moment.

Detachment

Don Juan places the utmost importance on the courage and solitary meditation needed to choose the path of heart. The only way to make this decision is to be free of fear and ambition and to have the wisdom of an old person. The crucial question is whether or not a path has heart, because if it does, you are on the right track. If it doesn't, it is of no use. One path makes you happy and strong, while the other weakens you.

The path of heart makes you feel strong and happy about your life because it follows your dreams, your dreamingbody, your mythical task. The other path is linked mainly to your primary processes, your old identity and its rigidly programmed doings. On this path, you become moody and complain; you feel like the victim of your path, sacrificing yourself for others.

The path of heart is a fluid path without rigid identities. It is the ancient Chinese Way, the Tao. It is water. It is formless and has no plans but flows wherever a passage opens up for it. The warrior on the path of heart is like a flute that lets the wind blow through it, making its own music.

You alone can make the decision about the path of heart, because in order to follow the dreamingbody, only you can perceive of and feel it. Your old age will help you remember that nothing is more important. After all, you own nothing but your own inner impulses. Your perceptions are the only things that really belong to you. Perhaps only old age relativizes the importance you place on other people's opinions and enables you to realize that the most important thing you can do is to value what you sense. You suffer if your path has too little heart, and deep down you have a sense of living senselessly.

I have had to leave a path without heart several times without tools or courage. Each time has been a struggle. Such changes require clarity and the ruthlessness that comes from inner certainty, characteristics of which I did not have enough.

The first time I consciously left a path was when I was in my teens and left a woman I was with because I knew the relationship would not work out. Later on, I had to do the same in other relationships, and though I was older, it was no easier. Once, getting on the path of heart meant changing my profession from physics to psychology; later I changed the particular method of psychology that I studied. Each change felt like a matter of life or death. Each time I hoped that this would be the last time I would have to make such a change. I barely realized that the path I was yearning for was an ever-changing one.

Since at this point in your apprenticeship you always seem to lack both the warrior's discipline and the Taoist's heart, you wonder if it is at all possible to live the dreaming-body in the real world. Is the path of heart only attainable when you are alone, with a master, or in therapy? Can it be lived in the city?

Don Juan tells Castaneda at this point that the busy street outside the house they have been in has been Castaneda's world, his "hunting ground."[2] Since no one escapes the doings of that world, the warrior reverses his attitude and makes every bit of this modern world useful. In Zen, this would be the moment when the second training begins, when the monk has finished his time in the monastery and is ready for the world. It is the moment when you receive a diploma. The time has come to live what you have learned. The Native American spiritual tradition accepts this moment as the right one, the only possible one. All the worlds are here, now. There is no heaven or earth outside of this moment.

If you view the world from the path of heart, you understand it to be the place to be for the moment, the place that you need in order to grow. The world is awful and awesome; from the viewpoint of the path of heart, what happens is meant to be used, completely and fully; dreamtime governs it. The world is not just an ordinary reality; it is the universe, a village where we all struggle together to find our entire selves. Here is where you find your greatest teachers, your body, your relationships, your dreams, your environment. Where else can you become yourself but in the wilderness with cougars and bears or in the city with battles, drugs, and the dangers of everyday life?

But the master's teachings are always somehow incongruent. They speak about living the nagual in everyday life, yet they always seem to take place mainly in an ashram or a wilderness. Most masters do not work in town. Most will not run for political office. Perhaps that is why you vote so rarely.

Why do great teachers live only in our dreams or in seclusion? Why does their path of heart take them into the mountains or into an ashram? Is it because they do not value ordinary life? Or is it that some teachings do not deal with relationships, everyday life, and today's world? Perhaps we must become the new teachers, who sit in the midst of a fist-fight or a race riot and claim that this is the right hunting ground. Teachers who say that fights are bad, that people should not riot, and that the city is somehow wrong may simply mean that, like us, they do not know how to deal with the world as it is.

Castaneda's teachers try to balance the dichotomy between journeying into foreign dimensions and living on the street by explaining how painful it is to have immense inner experiences and then to go back home again. To a person having a powerful experience, home sometimes seems like the wrong place to be. Everyone seems materialistic. Castaneda makes the Yaqui teachers sound like many spiritual teachers who consider our everyday selves to be unenlightened idiots.

Before you have to deal with an ally, the world consists of predictable events and situations that are difficult and un-avoidable. After you recognize the ally and the dreaming-body, the world from which you have come seems limited, and people there seem to be cut off from life. The integration of the ally and the creation of the double change you abruptly.

But this change is not permanent. The tendency to return to the home from which you have come means that you, too, are an ordinary person; otherwise, you would not still love much of what you left there. Some of your old feelings persist, though you can no longer identify with that world. Change happens so rapidly that you barely have time to grow older and allow its ruthlessness to transform your old self. It is as if you are half-cooked; part of you follows fate, while the other still longs for an imagined golden age.

So you first go backward in your attempt to live your full self. You return to rediscover the world and begin by thinking you have to enlighten others. This is a lonely moment, in which you find yourself sitting with old friends whom you no longer know. The problem is that the others are attached to things that you have partially dropped. And so you find yourself laughing quietly and alone at things others are not interested in.

But this loneliness is a sign that you have more work to do, for abrupt changes take years to digest. Integrating the ally means living the double all the time. Jung describes the pain and loneliness of this period: "There was a daimon in me, and in the end its presence proved decisive. It overpowered me, and if I was at times ruthless it was because I was in the grip of the daimon. I could never stop at anything once attained. I had to hasten on, to catch up with my vision. Since my contemporaries, understandably, could not perceive my vision, they saw only a fool rushing ahead."[3]

Even more painful, perhaps, is that you cannot understand yourself during these times. You are compulsive, driven, irritated by others, and still lonely and impatient. The madness of the ally is still around, pressing you to live and express its message. The car in front of you is always in the way. Why must you wait so long to get the overview you need to support your impossible self in the world?

Jung delineates the way in which the ally separated him from others: "I know things and must hint at things which others apparently know nothing of, and for the most part do not want to know. Loneliness does not come from having no people about one but from being unable to communicate the things that seem important to oneself, or from holding certain views which others find inadmissible. . . . If a man knows more than others, he becomes lonely."[4] Ordinary people seem like phantoms to you as you sense more of your dreaming-body. You cannot share your ideas and activities because they seem inadmissible secondary processes, city shadows for the culture that you are living in. For this reason, one nagual looks for another to feel at one with. You look no longer for an ordinary relationship, but for one chosen or revealed by the path of heart.

Today, there may be more support and empathy for visions of allies and the shaman's training than there were at earlier periods in history. Who knows? In any case, we find ourselves living at the beginning of a new century, at a time when democracy is struggling for rebirth, when alternative and shamanistic thinking are becoming almost mainstream. Yet there will never be an agreement on how to live the double in everyday life. For those on the path of heart, existence will always happen at the periphery of what others call life.

As Jung wrote, the pain of loneliness is balanced by the magical experience of the double, of living with a "secret, a premonition of things unknown. It fills life with something impersonal, a numinosum. A man who has never experienced that has missed something important. He must sense that he lives in a world which in some respects is mysterious; that things happen and can be experienced which remain inexplicable; that not everything which happens can be anticipated. The unexpected and the incredible belong to this world. Only then is life whole. For me, the world has from the beginning been infinite and ungraspable."[5]

What could Jung's secret have been? Some have speculated about extramarital affairs. Jung's political views were naive, even impossible. Though he was widely respected, he was also widely disliked, perhaps misunderstood by many of his contemporaries. Some envisioned him as a mystic or a madman. Don Juan was aware of how culture misunderstands the shaman. He said that a man of knowledge should erase his personal history so that the thoughts of others would not kill him.

Perhaps you can never completely return to the town and the people you have loved, for you no longer contribute congruently to the old belief system, its cultural rules, and its superstitions. Your sense of your body and of dreamtime hinders you from arriving in the twenty-first century. Your spirit makes you uncomfortable as long as you act like others. You try to perform the doings of reality, but something in you grieves and searches for that mysterious thing that makes life worthwhile. You lament your losses, because your new ground is not solid enough to stand on yet. You may even dream that all who have loved you have passed away while your spirit has wandered nostalgically in a regression. At this point in Castaneda's apprenticeship, his development and the world seem incommensurable. His innerwork remains separate from the world outside.

Shamanic studies need to deal with exactly what happens when you come back to town, how people react, and how you interact with them. Interaction with the world is a new stage in shamanism that we must all develop together.

EXERCISES

1. Describe your momentary path in life. Feel it. Does it give you joy, or does it weaken you? What part exhausts or bores you? Notice where you are living. Is this the right place? Imagine, if possible, using the present path to grow more. Don't work at trying; just see if growing more comes easily.

2. Drop the path without heart. If you are happy with your path, it is the path of heart; otherwise, it is not. If it is not the right path, or if you need help leaving elements of your present path that are not right for you, consider the following:

Imagine that you are very old, wise, and heartfelt. Advise yourself about your path. Are you doing too much of one thing and not enough of another? Feel and imagine a heartfelt way to leave your path if it is without heart.

Some inner figures might resist your path of heart. If you yourself are one of these people, go back to your personal history and notice the change that must happen in your identity for you to live on the path of heart. Outer people also resist your changing to a path with more heart. Imagine them now. Imagine changes in their world that, in your mind, should happen because of your changes. What meaning could your new path possibly have for others? Imagine these people and discuss it with them in your mind.

3. Move onto the path of heart. Pretend for a moment at least that you are free, old, and detached, and humbly follow what life wants from you. Pretend that you have the courage to change and that you are doing so now. Imagine that you are on the path of heart. Tell a friend about this path and how you got there.

2

DREAMING
IN THE CITY

CHAPTER 11

DEATH
OR
SORCERY

The body wants to dream. It needs to reduce stress and also to become the creator of trouble. It wants to live at the edge of the unknown and gets weak if it is only protected or "healthy." The dreamingbody requires more than wellness; it wants challenge, risk, personal power, and freedom. Even more than this, the body must seek danger in order to become itself. The dreamingbody will never be healed through healthy living alone, because it seeks the uncanny, at the edge, through dreaming. Don Juan puts it dramatically when he says that the body loves terror and darkness and gains personal power from these elements.[1]

Your body is on a creative journey. In your fantasies, dreams, and reality, you return to magical places, moments, and teachers who have given you access to power. You review problems and traumas and experiment with ecstasy in your dreams, not only to untie the knots of your personal development, but to search for increasingly difficult tasks and experiences. The ability to be yourself requires more than self-knowledge; it is a matter of loving, struggling, failing, and rising again.

Therefore, after powerful inner experiences, you return home, not only for sentimental reasons, but because this everyday life is as much a wilderness as the forest is. Today, shamanism must deal with a world on fire, one huge, hot greenhouse, troubled democracies, and impossible relationships. This world is part of everyone's path of heart, and everyone around you seeks transformation. Returning to the everyday world not only reconnects you to what you have left behind, it reminds you of what was boring and painful and catapults you into a life-and-death conflict: living with the nagual in the city.

Your home challenges you to realize your visions in everyday life. But since your experiences may conflict with the lives of others, everyone will have to change. And as we all change, we in turn transform shamanism, for its ancient setting is no more. Forgetting shamanism will never work, because psychology and medicine become one-dimensional without their ancient sister. Thus, shamanism will have to play a major role in reshaping our helping professions.

Therapy and Sorcery

As shamanism confronts psychology, therapy will become more community oriented, heartful, and magical. At present, medicine and therapy value the average person and aim at survival. The sorcerer focuses on the quality of life and improvises as she goes along. The world of the sorcerer is madness and magic, while at worst therapy seeks to tame your demons or at least to explain them so that you will be able to fit in with others.

From the present viewpoint, it would seem that therapy was developed to support the worldview of the middle classes. It is available to those who have the money, time, and security for introspection. It takes you to the door of other worlds, senses and explains what is on the other side, and closes the door again. Therapy grasps the life of the average person and focuses on how to make it more secure. Stop your addictions, don't be abusive, increase your self-esteem, know your anima and animus, don't get into trouble with your clients, don't be codependent, act like others, and choose a partner of the opposite sex.

The more adventurous methods sniff at the door to the other world or cross over for short periods of time but recommend consensus white reality as the measure for what is good. Look at dreams, feel and understand the body, and find the missing feeling in relationships, and the world ought to be in order again. Except that it is not. Something big is missing. There is no jazz, no color, nothing interesting happening in the community.

Sorcery adds another dimension to the work. Like the therapist, the sorcerer opens the door to the other world, but unlike the therapist, the sorcerer follows her ally and goes on. A sorcerer's life is not complete until she goes through the door to the unknown and keeps going until the wall between the worlds disappears. The sorcerer's world has no doors, few boundaries, and no opposites in it. She dances until she is exhausted, not until she finds the meaning. She does not "integrate" parts of her unconscious or study herself; she follows her body.

Being an average person, sorcerer, warrior, hunter, or therapist is a matter of timing. All are aspects of one another. If you are a sorcerer, life is art, poetry, and madness. You perform a script that is written as you act. If you are a therapist, you study the script and the actress, asking what it all means for tomorrow.

Shamanism adds spice to personal transformation, just as therapy gives modern shamans a way to earn a living. The therapist pays attention to the forgotten, the sorcerer to the ridiculous. The sorcerer gladly runs into trouble because of her love for the absurd. She nourishes the thief, the liar, and the lunatic.

While madness is the shadow problem of therapists who fear insanity, the warrior shaman nourishes the uncanny. He re-envisions madness as a gift to be developed, an emergence of the spirit. Just as death is the warrior's adviser, craziness should be the therapist's.

Many therapies were developed to work with the middle classes. They support the normative values of dominant cultures: family, work, education, knowledge, health, sanity, and everyday life. They stress insight and personal growth, life and happiness. Yet they seem to ignore prejudice, economic disparity, and violent racial conflicts.

The sorcerer is different. Until recently, she was rarely middle class, and she dealt with death as well as life, voodoo, and love. The shaman worried about the sustainability of her community and cared for it by dealing with spirits in the air. If the life of an individual is the implicit goal of therapy, then death, the mystery of darkness, and community renewal are the realm of the sorcerer.

Death

When your brain is sufficiently dead, people of Western thinking gather around your body and pronounce you dead. That's it for you. You get the red light. If you end up in a coma beforehand, people will be nice to you, but they really think you are not around. Those who have not worked with comatose states or with the Tibetan or Egyptian Books of the Dead say that you don't exist in a coma. If you look like a vegetable and don't talk, you have no personality. Where do they think you went?

Our twenty-first-century world dislikes introverts and fantasy-full states so much that when your time has come to die, you may even feel guilty. The message you will get from everyone is, "Do everything, but for god's sake, don't be a loser and die!"

That is why you feel awful when you get sick. Not because you are ill, but because you feel like a loser. Everyone treats you as if you don't have a dreamingbody. No one listens to your dreams. Yet most people are very busy with living at the point of death. Everyone I have worked with reflects what Elisabeth Kubler Ross said years ago, that near-death people are focused upon learning and loving. Why not? The fact that you are ninety-five doesn't mean you can't have an affair. And people do have affairs in their "final" dreamingbody experiences. I expect that, as this information becomes more widely known, conferences for the so-called dying on shamanism, relationship, and dreaming will become mainstream.

In any case, while everyone else is running from death, the shaman immerses himself in it in order to live life more fully. Therapists feel obliged to preserve consciousness, to classify and eradicate pathological aberrations. The sorcerer, on the other hand, respects death, as does the Buddhist who reaches enlightenment through meditating upon his demise.

The shaman in you lives daily with the sense of death, while the rest of you fights the depressing thought that life will soon be over. I think it is as the shamans say: Only the sense of imminent death shakes you loose from your momentary attachments and fears, from your interest in the programs you have set up. And so the sorcerer welcomes death as the end to a lifestyle that has long since run out of steam. The shaman finds transformation and ecstasy—not tragedy or failure—in death.

Controlled Abandon

If the relationship between psychology and shamanism goes well, both will nourish each other. The sorcerer isn't perfect, and the ideal shaman must master more of the world. We need teachers to model living on the path of heart and meeting the ally in the city, in relationships. The shaman knows that the ally is not just the spirit chasing her in the wilderness. But moving from the ally in the wilderness to a burglar at the front door requires rethinking.

Therapy has a lot to learn from shamanism, especially around the area of the second attention. Here is finally the name for the ability to stay with and focus on experiences that you normally ignore. Any therapy that deals with the unconscious looks infantile in this realm compared to the Yaqui Way of Knowledge.

Developing the second attention requires focusing on subtle signals for extended periods of time while retaining access to ordinary reality. This is a matter of abandon and control, of abandoning your identity and controlling the evolution of processes by following them intently. The more you experience and know about these states, the more control you have while in them.

Controlled abandon is a useful concept necessary for working with altered states of consciousness. Therapists who help people near death or in comas, or who help people to develop their total selves, will need the shaman's viewpoint. You can begin with dreams, body experiences, relationships, movement, the world, or internal dialogue. Notice what happens, keep control over your awareness, and let go.

Some cultures teach the second attention more than others do. Many of our Japanese students had a lot of controlled abandon. Amy and I worked with a doctor while we were in Tokyo who was fascinated by one of his dreams, which he interpreted as indicating old age and death. In his dream, one animal had been slowly eating another animal to death. He told this dream and asked what it meant in the midst of a seminar. We were all standing in a circle.

"Am I going to die?" he asked. I didn't know, but I said that his process would interpret the dream. I thought that if the spirit created the dream, then it would have to interpret it as well. We agreed to use our second attentions on whatever dreaming process would emerge.

We stood facing one another. His face became tense, and he suddenly complained about his rapidly, irregularly pounding heart. Sweating and confused, he asked me what to do. I replied that since his heartbeat had come to his attention, this process would show us the way. "Let's use controlled aban-don and follow that irregular heart." Hesitantly, he experi-mented with walking around the room to the rhythm of his heart. He stomped as if he were a pounding heart and loudly and clearly pronounced his discovery: "I am in the military." I asked him if the military were at war with something. In a powerful general's voice, he boomed, "The military is at war with responsibility! It hates responsibility and refuses to be eaten alive by it! The war is with responsibility!" This insight had an amazing effect on him. He leapt for joy, left the circle of participants, and sat down. Everyone clapped with enthusi-asm, but, to tell the truth, I don't think anyone, including me, really knew why. It took us fifteen minutes to catch up with his instantaneous enlightenment.

The doctor's second attention had explained his dream to him. He was being eaten alive by responsibility and was not following his heart. His heart had become a warrior, showing him how to react to a life without freedom. I was amazed, however, at his ability to let go and follow the river of dreams.

To understand dreams, you need the shaman's con-trolled abandon to let the river of dreams explain itself. The sorcerer in you seeks contact with the awesome and numinous, not with rational insight. The contact itself brings what Zen calls "satori," or sudden awakening from direct experience.

The shaman shares certain characteristics with the Zen master and the Taoist priest; you will need these characteris-tics in working on yourself. Therapy and self-transformation happen best because of the way you work, not because of what you do. Concepts like the second attention and con-trolled abandon come out of the context of the crazy wisdom teacher, the part of you that is open to nature, that has no-where to go but follows the streams and impulses of the mo-ment. The attitude you have in working with yourself and others needs as much attention as the issues at stake.

In any case, interpreting dreams interests the mind, for-wards your understanding, and enriches normal existence, but it does not necessarily awaken your body. If you integrate dreamwork with shamanism, dreams become an invitation to altered states of consciousness. On the other hand, if you integrate psychology with shamanism, you can drum to enter trance states, find lost souls in other worlds with dreaming, and find these same states peeping out of your own double signals.

Partners as Naguals

How does shamanism work on relationships? Since every healer is different, this question can never be answered. However, the goal of the shaman is to journey through altered states to find solutions. This leads to the realization that you can never completely know who you are or with whom you are living. What happens when two people live their dreamingbodies together is even less describable than when one lives it alone.

If you and your partner simultaneously use your second attention, you stop the world, you change it. You might turn into wild animals or distinguished royalty, lovers or fighters, depending upon your process. Central American shamans might call you a "nagual woman" and a "nagual man."

I remember a couple whom Amy and I worked with. Jan was upset with Donald because he always talked about other women. She told us that every time they took a walk, he would flirt with a passing woman. Donald admitted that this was true and that he, too, was upset about his behavior. Amy turned the whole thing around. She told both of them to focus their second attention upon the unknown, the ghost between them. Amy explained that the woman Donald talked about was a secondary process, an ally that was constantly disturbing the relationship.

The couple did not seem to get the idea, so I encouraged them to use their second attention and controlled abandon and imagine this other woman. They focused on her, and then Donald found what it was that excited him. "Oh," he said, "she's so romantic." Before Jan had a chance to react, Amy told Donald to practice controlled abandon and become this woman. To everyone's surprise, Donald actually became what he imagined the other woman to be. He spoke and moved passionately and romantically. That was all they needed. Jan was so excited by this new behavior that she embraced him, saying that a romantic husband is exactly what she wanted. The "other woman" was the couple's ally, a troublesome figure disturbing both of them. This figure was a preview of Donald's double signals and his wife's greatest hope.

The ally, then, is a shared phenomenon that everyone needs. But to get to this dimension of relationship, you and your friends need to be nagual people and accept the spirit, using second attention and controlled abandon.

Shamanism not only *enriches* relationship, it *is* relationship. Dreaming together is a core experience that binds people together; it was the center of tribal culture. Without it, relationships can be loving, compassionate, secure, or troublesome, but not amazing. Together, we spin worlds that are difficult to maintain alone.

Caretaker of the Absurd

More than anything else, the sorcerer is the essential aspect of self-transformation. With some coaxing, the sorcerer can teach the therapist how to make the profession worth practicing by being the caretaker for the absurd. He turns things around and transforms difficult events into fun.

We all sense strange little symptoms and sometimes life-threatening problems in our bodies. While the therapist in you tries to heal these problems, the sorcerer looks for the virtual realities, the world in which symptoms survive.

This reminds me of Karen, a woman I worked with once who was in her last stages of cancer. One day several weeks before she died, she was sitting in her wheelchair and could barely speak. The pain was intense and exhausting, and she had no energy to walk. Yet when she coughed or tried to speak, the slightest smile could be seen at the corners of her mouth. I asked her about what I thought might be a smile, and she assured me that she was smiling for no reason. "I've gone through all the treatments," she said, "and I am refusing any-more help. I'm in the pre-dying stage." She smiled some more.

I used my second attention to focus on that seemingly irrational signal. "I love your smile," I said. "It gives me the sense that you have already died." But I was wrong; she did not identify with that signal. In fact, she became more serious and said that she was not happy. "I want to get happy before I die," she said. "That's why I'm here."

Instead of insisting that she be serious and face her death, I decided to take another route. "Others might notice you are already happy and wonder how you could laugh at such a time. Where does your sense of humor come from?" I asked.

Karen looked at me, confused. "Hmmm, well . . . why should I be miserable?" she asked and smiled again. "I am looking forward to dying." I could not help but encourage that little smile. "I see that you've already gotten one of the big keys to life: grinning and having a good time."

That must have been powerful for her, for she looked at me with tears in her eyes. "You make me cry with happiness," she said. "You see something in me that nobody else sees."

Then she explained to me that this was her second bout with cancer. She had waited too long to go to the surgeon be-cause she loathed conventional medical institutions. Finally, she had decided to start a vigorous treatment against the can-cer, but it was too late. She said that everyone had criticized her for her negligence.

I looked at her and said, "They didn't understand that you were risking your life to take an alternative route. And they couldn't see that, in some way, death is a friend."

She agreed. "Yes," she said with excitement, "Death could stop me from hurting, and death could help me to free my spirit."

I asked her where her spirit would go once it was free. Karen thought for a second and said, "It would have fun! You know," she confessed, "I don't really want to get well. I would have too many problems. I'm sick and tired of them."

"Great," I said, "Let's just die to all your problems." I felt guilty about feeling so well at a moment like this, but I remembered my own shaman teachers from Africa. It seemed to me that their love for the uncanny, their second attention and abandonment, were there to help Karen and me drop our personal history and seriousness about dying.

I suggested that, even though Karen was in a wheelchair, we might work with movement. I told her to follow whatever happened. She agreed and tried to stand, though she had to bend over because the tumors in her spine made it impossible for her to stand straight. I asked her to focus upon her bent position without judgments, to find out what it felt like to stand in a bent position. She said her position gave her the impression that she was an ape—an ape beginning a race. Where was the race going, I wanted to know. She roared with laughter and told me it was going nowhere. She said she was just being an ape having a good time.

This ape was her ally, her gait of power. The ape was her double. "Your body is supporting your nature, showing you how to fool around, how to start a race and not even worry about completing it." She wept with happiness and cried out that life was truly absurd. She had always been so serious and demanded of herself that whatever she started she must finish. Laughing, she said that now that we had started, we were also finished with our work. That was her last dance, her way of teaching all those who witnessed that enjoying the race, the process of transformation, was the important thing. It doesn't make any difference if you finish; the important thing is to get started.

EXERCISES

1. Consider a relationship problem that you have had recently. What part of you does the other person criticize? Try getting back into that relationship, but this time, do something absurd. Experiment with your second attention. Become the part or characteristic that the other criticizes. Let go of your personal history and experiment with enjoying it.

Now use this critical part of yourself independently of that relationship. Use it practically for yourself and others. Your partner must have been seeing an ally that was far from your awareness.

2. Imagine for a moment that you have permission to go crazy. Notice how you feel. What do you look like? Now imagine using this madness in your relationships. Don't only try to get them in order, but stir up a little trouble. Do something awesome instead of waiting for life to do something to you.

ARNOLD MINDELL

CHAPTER 12

DREAMING TOGETHER

When you consider your friends to be warriors in a shamanic clan, you become teachers to one another, and your group becomes the nagual. This is one way to integrate shamanistic teachings into group life.

Think of Castaneda. At one point in his apprenticeship, he tells the story of being challenged by an apprentice with whom he has been flirting. As the two near her bed, she turns and almost kills the unwitting apprentice. She blasts him out of his unconsciousness and wakens him to lucid dreaming. In fact, all of Castaneda's colleagues are awesome and worthy opponents at one moment or another, supporting, teaching, and challenging each other. They are naguals for each other. They are wild, yet heartful; solitary warriors, yet immensely interactive with one another. Their relationship styles are uncanny, because they are being themselves and facilitating each others' transformation.

Shamans' stories are filled with lessons about how warrior clans develop. Such groups are organized by a common interest in awareness, a drive that operates decisively but mysteriously in the background of relationships. Though Castaneda did not stress the community element in his teachings, the traditions he reports on clearly have much to teach us about creating and sustaining a lively and meaningful community life.

The implicit lessons are that no one succeeds in consciousness unless everyone does and that your warrior colleagues are as important as your teachers in your learning. The image of the solitary warrior in don Juan's stories is magnificent, but it makes no sense without a warrior clan. A group of warriors behaves like an interdependent network of awareness enthusiasts. Each one takes the next as a friend, partner, and worthy opponent. To be a warrior means to be your true self, that is, to be difficult, loving and playing tricks on your friends to help both them and yourself to awareness. Don Juan even admits how important his apprentices are to him. After all, Castaneda's stubbornness has forced don Juan to grow as an effective teacher.

As indigenous tribal life is breaking apart under the impact of modern technology, shamanism is not just fading away and becoming a dreamlike relic of the past. It reemerges in the myth of awareness and challenges us to become our maximum selves. Everyone is dying to live ecstatically in a community where spirits and people are equal. Without shamanlike interactions based upon the second attention, individual and community life is incomplete. Your community would be a dull place without unpredictable spirits and worthy opponents forcing you to become whole.

Mombasa

When Amy and I travel to foreign countries, we frequently seek out indigenous communities and their witch doctors to help us understand the ways the spirit moves in the places we work. I especially remember the experience we had in a ceremony with two Kenyan healers, on the east Indian coast of Kenya, near Mombasa.

The ceremony began when we first landed in Mombasa. I asked one of the employees at the hotel where we were staying to take us to a witch doctor. He hesitated and then told us that his uncle would see us the next day.

When the time came, we drove our rented car along rough dirt roads, in the heat of the equatorial Kenyan bush, to meet the witch doctor. Each mile we drove carried us deeper into the spirit of Kenya and further from our ordinary reality. We parked near a mud hut and were immediately surrounded by the entire village of people.

Inside the hut, sitting cross-legged on the earthen floor, were a husband and wife team of witch doctors. The man was a body healer, the woman a seer. On the wall hung old yellowing and worn certificates, in English, attesting that they were witch doctors. Our healer couple spoke only Swahili. It was a pleasure to meet these quiet and reserved people who worked as laborers by day and as magicians by night.

They were at once impeccable hosts, ordinary people, and mystics. They treated us with innocence and extreme humility. They took our hands, welcomed us into their tribe, and spent hours exchanging our Western clothes for simple and colorful cloth. They wrapped the cloth around our naked bodies and proclaimed, in a very special moment, "Now you are African." Their openness healed a problem I had been unaware of, a disease I did not know I had. Deep inside of me was a longing, making me half ill. I had forgotten that I had wished the world I lived in would give me this sense of belonging. I had been made to feel guilty for not participating in some groups; I had felt loved in other groups, but none had given me the sense that I was crucial to its well-being.

In any case, when the ceremony began, Amy and I sat quietly in a small group of people made up of the husband and wife team, her friends or sisters, and various stragglers from the village, who were there for unknown reasons. The woman healer read from some holy book, perhaps the Koran. As she read, she half sang and, after a few minutes, fell into a trance and began rolling on the floor, allowing herself to follow her dreamingbody. We were the clients of sorcerers who were plummeting into the depths of our souls and bodies. After having cared for so many others, we were more than touched by the manner in which the entire community was now gathering as the ceremony went on to support us. Even the little children were there, the ones who would take our hands the next day and proudly show us their swimming hole, a river filled with wild animals and vegetation foreign to us. As the healers sang and rolled, I felt supported and renewed in my work.

The psychological community I had grown up in looked down upon therapists interested in group experience, and so, in my own weakness, I had felt guilty about occasionally inviting group participation in my work with individuals. Now I realized how important this participation was. The older tribeswomen held our hands in the evening darkness, comforting us before we met with the unknown. The dim light of their torches filled the hut with love and companionship. The whole village took part, appearing with somber and respectful faces, all expecting to be healed by whatever would happen.

As the witch doctors sang and danced, two "sisters" who had up until then been quiet participants from the circle rolled forward into the center, moving ecstatically in trance states. The healers changed visage as they journeyed into unknown spaces. They let their own processes direct them as they moved unpredictably around the circle. While the woman sang and moaned, the man moved rapidly and unpredictably about, his psychic hands performing surgery on passive clients, using a quick, sharp knife that drew things from their bodies without making one incision or bringing out one drop of blood.

We were awestruck, terrified at his dexterity but also relieved to be in a place so weird that it felt like home. We shall never know exactly what the others suffered from. All I know is that I was sick at heart from a lack of connection to the invisible. Our bodies needed that ceremony honoring the spirit, the second attention, the unusual, the uncanny.

To remember myself, I need contact with my African sisters and brothers, with Native American traditions, Japanese masters, Indian teachers, and aboriginal diviners. The body needs awesome experience, fear, and the power that comes from a loving community. Without such experience, ordinary life misses something that affirms its reason for existence.

The capacity of this couple to perform miraculous healings was impressive, but the most healing thing was their worldview, which placed the uncanny in the center of community life. All of us are burdened with problems that cannot easily be solved. Yet we hide these problems or feel inferior because of them and relegate the spirit to visions of the night.

Today, modern Africans living in big cities like Nairobi are embarrassed by their native healers and hesitate to mention them, though many still believe in them. Yet we all need these healers, more than ever. Without them, we tend to forget and are embarrassed about our secret connection to the uncanny spirit of life. And community life needs the spirit that, through the figure of shamans, centers it and facilitates its core experience, healing its members through dreaming together.

Shamans heal by reminding you of the dreamingbody. They model awareness and the dance of the spirit. Archaic systems of ecstasy, the community's living center, give a village its life. The tradition of community healing, the idea that one person's suffering is part of the whole community, creates human warmth and contact. Without such trance dancers, a group of people becomes an abstract and meaningless entity, a city whose members are obligated to fulfill empty duties. No one can lead a meaningless life for long or tolerate cities with no purpose.

A New View of Your Home Town

In a shaman's view of the city, the spirit is everywhere, waiting to dance. The shaman would advise you not to feel badly if the people around you at work seem boring or impossible; like wild animals, they are the spirits that provoke you to reach your own totality. By running into trouble with others, you are forced to plumb the depths of yourself.

Aboriginal bush is full of spirits, but your present city is full of neglected ghosts as well. The world is filled with people and forces whose signals go unseen or unheeded. Each community dreambody is composed of people, things, and spirits. Daily business consists not only of people trying to make money, but of warriors struggling for freedom.

This may be why you have strange dreams about your colleagues and why you hope in vain that leaders or managers will be warriors, teachers, or priestesses. You search for a new world, a place where enlightenment is the background process trying to happen in daily business. In this ordinary and special place, you and all those around you are dreaming, trying to find the path of heart and an ally within existing tension and relationship conflicts. Today's city is populated not only by people but by lost and naked powers shifting aimlessly through the streets. In sections of the city where crime and violence rule, you have to develop your shaman's body to survive. In conflict areas, no one succeeds unless everyone does.

A recent conference in Oregon comes to mind. Several hundred people from all over the world had convened to study conflict resolution—how to get along with one another. I especially remember the seminar's beginning.

Things had become suddenly intense when someone criticized the conference organizers for advertising certain events that they were unable to stage at the conference. The critics made their point, and the organizers apologized. Yet the conflict dragged on for some reason. Suddenly, an African American stood up and loudly called for his "forty acres and a mule." The room froze.

Though this conference took place in the United States, few knew that the U.S. government had promised each freed slave forty acres and a mule after the American Civil War but had never fulfilled that promise. Back we went into the unfinished business of the earlier time. The conference became a community as it switched gears, so to speak, putting its second attention on the issue of racial repression and the conflict between the U.S. government, white Americans, and African Americans. The African Americans wanted the debt repaid.

With the surfacing of this tense interracial conflict, seemingly out of nowhere, the original conflict about the organization disappeared. It was a year before the citizen demonstrations in Los Angeles, where African Americans rioted in response to unfair treatment, yet the organization's broken promise was like a catalyst, plummeting us into the different reality that the whole nation would experience a year later. A futurist or a witch doctor might say that the African American had followed his shaman's body, putting us all where we needed to be, in the pain and trauma of racial inequality and injustice.

Various opinions, feelings, and positions were expressed, but the issue was not relieved until someone stepped into the African American position and spoke movingly and congruently about the pain of being an African American in white America. "Many of you have suffered at the hands of your parents and are still complaining about that today. No? Then don't expect an abused person whose race has been oppressed for centuries to stop complaining. The suffering we blacks have endured is ancient. And we are still in pain and anger today, not only for the past, but because right now everyone in this room thinks that we should forget our pain and move on. We are angry because everyone hates listening to pain and no one is prepared to pay what is due."

That did it. Everyone understood that the African Americans' pain, everyone's pain, comes not only from the past, but from the present, in the way we all ignore suffering and criticize the sufferer for not progressing beyond pain. Only when you accept pain and change its source in the present can you move on.

Until that person spoke about the agony of the African Americans, pain had been a forbidden subject. But as soon as it was represented, it was no longer a disavowed and hungry ghost, but a living spirit that animated and unified. In that moment, everyone was ill, and at the same time, something was healed. Everyone belonged to the same tribe, and all of us were warriors focusing our second attention on the world as we dreamed together.

Shortly thereafter, another problem arose. Several Jewish women took issue with a participant who had been in Hitler's army during the Second World War. The man defended himself as best he could but finally admitted that he loved Hitler because Hitler had promised the German people a way out of misery and poverty. "Hitler showed the strength no one else had to break the depression of the Treaty of Versailles," he said. This man's love for Hitler split the group, and its dreamingbody became the Second World War. People took sides and spoke in anger and pain. Some became so furious that they threatened to lynch the man, while others pleaded for mercy.

Many people, especially people of European background, don't like conflict and try to avoid it. Thus, the kind of development in which so much pain and conflict arises is the kind that many shun. Yet you unconsciously want conflict; you know it is present, and that is why war has been so central to many cultures for thousands of years. It is one of the few things left in which everyone moves in a trance, together.

But there are better ways to "shoot straight" than with guns. A group in which everyone is in turmoil is like a world at war: The evil one is the enemy to be overcome. We tried to handle the conflict with Hitler's soldier in a civil manner. Some of us spoke for him, others against him. Yet there seemed no end in sight, because no one would admit that he or she had ever done or would ever do evil. Evil was a figment of everyone's imagination, a ghost projected onto this man like a spirit in the air. The man gave adequate reason for this projection at that time. Yelling at him, however, would not kill prejudice, nor would his punishment bring back the dead.

Finally a Swiss man developed his second attention, noticed the missing secondary process—the group soul—and went deeply into it. He spoke with tears in his eyes. "I am a guilty one," he said to everyone. "I was a child of Swiss parents who lived during the Second World War, and some of my people supported Hitler by turning Jews away at the border. Many who were turned back entered concentration camps and were killed. How can I ever repay the world for the fact that I am guilty by implication? I am guilty, very guilty."

His expression of guilt and sadness broke the spell. That group came together because someone's second attention and controlled abandon led us to the missing ghost. Someone must take responsibility for the problems of today and yesterday; otherwise, evil is a disembodied ghost. This huge community shrank in size and became intimate, for the moment, at least.

The world that dreams together becomes a community if someone with a shaman's body steps over a cultural edge and ventures out, with controlled abandon, into the unknown. That person must use her second attention and ability to dream together to help the town experience the unknown by letting it move her.

At that same conference, when the gays and lesbians spoke of having been brutally rejected by social rules, no one wanted to admit their prejudices or homophobic reactions to homosexual relationships. Finally, once again, someone found a part of himself that was homophobic and clearly stated that he was against gay people: He had the foolish prejudice that gays and lesbians were neurotic. This man dropped his personal history of being a liberal, alternative thinker and became the prejudice that was in the air.

He created violent reactions and a clearing. People spoke about prejudice and unconsciousness. Ideas about political change and homophobia arose. No solution could really occur without greater political awareness of the issues involved. Yet slowly that group of several hundred people began to feel like a town I could live in, a place where the unspoken could arise, where pain and suffering were present, heard, and felt. Just as our Mombasa healers had sought the troublesome spirits who were bothering us, this group sought impossible ghosts in its tense background. Dreaming together brings momentary unity out of diversity.

Unconscious figures, dreams, ghosts, and spirits come not only from human bodies, but also from the earth. We should expect genus loci spirits, or earth spirits, around the world to rebel as well. According to James Swan, in Delphi, Greece, where Gaia was worshiped in ancient times, an aluminum plant threatens to pollute the surroundings.[1] Indigenous tribes are upset about the dying spirit of the rainforests. The Masai are no longer allowed their rituals on Mount Kilamanjaro, in Tanzania, and Australian aborigines are angry that tourists can climb over their sacred rock, Uluru; after all, those same tourists would not climb on the roof of a church. Native Americans are fighting loggers because the U.S. and Canadian governments build roads over sacred Native territory.

For a sorcerer, the entire earth is a holy spot, which everyone else neglects. No one takes unpredictable earth events seriously enough. Not only is the environment neglected, but everywhere the spirit of the place goes unseen by the second attention. Even dirty streets in modern cities full of skyscrapers and filth, where millions must prepare their evening beds, can be places of power as well as caverns of abysmal suffering. Wherever you walk on earth, there is both the sacred and the mundane.

For instance, everyone is appalled by Bombay, a city with enormous suffering. Some corners of Bombay have so many people that Times Square, Manhattan, feels empty by comparison. Poverty-stricken people panhandle for money everywhere. According to the *India Times*, as many as fifteen thousand impoverished people from the countryside invade Bombay's slums per week at certain times of the year. The unhappy and poor street people of Bombay impinge upon tourists, who can survive there only briefly. The stench and wretchedness of certain corners is so intense that the only reasonable first reactions are philanthropy, dysentery, and horror.

Yet there is something in the steamy heat and smog of Bombay that affects you, something that gives you another viewpoint of the terrible poverty. In spite of the problems, or perhaps because of them, there is normally a surprising lack of violence on the city streets. The clash between Muslims and Hindus is changing this scene at present, yet why at other times has Bombay been so quiet? Is it the Indian philosophy of Karma? The concept of Karma can also lead to the kind of passivity that lets poverty happen.

But the Hindu scriptures have something more compelling than the laissez-faire attitude of Karma. India accepts the beggar as a demonstration of psychic and social problems, as a city shadow, a dramatic reminder of the effects of Karma. The message of the beggar is to "observe your life and improve your lot, or you, too, will look like this next time around."

I think the message is even more complex. Something special holds Bombay together. Amy and I had arrived there just after being in South Africa. The city's poverty was unbearable, but compared with what we had just seen in Cape Town—in 1990, before the apartheid state was dissembled—Bombay seemed happier, although poorer. Freedom plays a huge role in making people happy. Amy and I bathed in this freedom and let Bombay's field invade us. Living in Bombay meant letting our dreamingbodies merge with the problems but also with the powers of that ancient city.

While we were there, Amy came down with the most incredible heat rash we had ever seen. We decided to try dreambodywork on her welts before going to the hospital. She felt into her rash and experienced wild claws tearing at her skin. She saw a picture of a tiger, and as she moved and felt the tiger in her body, she realized that it contained her disavowed reactions to a particular street corner in Bombay, one that stank so much that she had gotten sick. With courage, she allowed herself to play the tiger, reacting against the stenches and finally transforming her reactions into a gloriously happy and ecstatic dance.

As she got into the heat rash, her ally, the tiger, emerged. Her skin felt better as she began to growl and to shout nasty, stinky opinions and thoughts that she had been repressing. She decided to share some of these thoughts with her friends in Bombay. Her relationships became temporarily impossible, but her welts drastically improved within minutes. That city was a hunting ground where she had found the monster Kali, the fierce goddess of the streets.

The Mahalakshmi Temple

The day Amy and I landed in Bombay, we were drowsy from jet lag, the change in altitude, and the smog. Without unpacking, we put on our running clothes and followed our trancelike state into the stream of people and traffic, down the most forbidding streets. Our dreamingbodies were our basic map, guiding us in the direction of least resistance and maximum danger.

We depended upon our bodies to find the most energizing and forbidding scenes as trail markers. Soon our run meandered through smoldering alleys to the sea, past screaming vendors and snake charmers. One snake enthusiast let her snake stick its head out and hiss at us. Our shudder indicated to us that this was the right track.

Where the alley suddenly opened onto the Arabian Sea, people were throwing flowers and fruits into the water as a sacrificial ritual. We watched, hiding behind the worshipers. In the distance, a strange old man with pure black skin, dressed all in white, with a shocking white beard, was waving at an invisible something in the air. His violent gestures matched his wild eyes. His motions were ecstatic as he continuously beckoned toward the sky. He was talking to himself. City life, as this man represented it, looked better to us with every moment.

I was staring at the man when he suddenly turned and looked back at me from a distance. I asked a worshiper who spoke English who the old man was. I was warned that he was a madman. I thought he looked magnificent. Someone like that would be arrested or put into a mental institution in Europe or the United States, but he looked no more dangerous than people I have worked with.

I wanted to meet him. The old man must have been telepathic, for he turned toward me at that moment and walked over to where we were standing. Perhaps he thought we were crazy, too. A worshiper near us timidly translated the old man's Hindi into English. Smiling broadly and waving his hands in dancing movements toward the sea, the man said, "The seas go out and the seas come in. Now it is high tide, soon it will be low. We must offer what we have to the Great One who lives not only in the sea but also beneath the ground and in the sky."

These statements not only convinced me that he was sane, but confirmed my original impression that there was something special about him. "God is all around," he bellowed in Hindi, gesturing with outstretched arms toward the heavens. "We sense that, too," I replied. After staring at us for a few moments, he said to the translator that he could see that we had our own spiritual tradition and yet followed the same gods as he. I mumbled in return that he must be a seer. "No," he insisted, continuing in the same vein. "My ears are Shiva's, and my eyes are the eyes of Shiva. I merely report on whatever I hear and see. It is not me, but god who speaks."

He said all this with his white garments blowing in the offshore wind on that hot day. He spoke with such genuineness and warmth, I felt the streets of Bombay had blessed us with a nagual, a wise teacher. He smiled and slowly turned his head upward, gesturing again to the skies. He laughed, and the world around him seemed to smile as he turned the chaos and clutter of Bombay into gold.

"All is Shiva," he said, and I understood that every business, group, and city is a spiritual experience waiting for our appreciation. As we left the shore, we found out from people on the streets that the spirit we had been following that day had brought us to the Mahalakshmi Temple and that he was its high priest.

"All is Shiva," the high priest had said. Community life, even the one you are in, is god as well. Shiva, god of awareness, is a picture of the earth's perception, the group mind of little gatherings and international conflicts, the global dreambody. The search for this body gives at least some meaning to madness and to the chaos around you. From this perspective, the world is mess, but it is also one immense warrior's clan, a madhouse in which we all disturb and provoke one another toward freedom.

EXERCISES

1. Consider dreaming together with your community and entering into a transformative group experience. Choose one of the groups you are in and ask yourself what feelings, thoughts, or moods you have about the group. Do you gossip about your friends there? What do you say in private about others?

2. Ghosts are aspects of people that you gossip about but that no one represents directly. Imagine a ghost, a figure behind

your own gossip. Imagine jealousy, power, ambition. How does your ghost look? Make your face look like its face. When are you possessed by this ghost?

3. What conflicts in your group related to this ghost are trying to surface?

4. Imagine that you or someone else plays this ghost during a meeting. What seems to happen? Are people surprised? Happy? Angry? Completely represent the forbidden ghost.

5. Now, as a creative possibility, see if you can consider that your group has another spirit, a mythic figure that is trying to awaken people. What might this spirit look like in your imagination?

6. Imagine your group coming together. Consider what it might look like if both the gossip ghost and the ghost that wants to awaken people were present. At least discuss these different spirits. Better yet, try dancing as these ghosts would. Experiment with moving and speaking like them, or present a short play. When you do this in public, ask others to join you in dreaming as you step into this dance. Some may dance the part of one ghost, some the other, and the ghosts may interact, conflict with each other, and play.

CHAPTER 13

PHANTOMS
AND
REAL PEOPLE

n chapter 1, I mentioned that don Juan tells Castaneda that the spirit determines how you identify yourself, whether you are an average person, a hunter, or a fluid warrior. Don Juan says that when you remove doubt about the reality of the spirit, the spirit changes, making it possible for you to use your second attention. It is finally up to the spirit to move your assemblage point, that is, the way in which you assemble or construct yourself. Without the help of the spirit, you may know about shamanism but be unable to use it in your life.

I experienced the spirit that moved me in a few of my teachers. They called themselves by different names. They were therapists, witch doctors, shamans, and gurus, yet they all played the crucial role of the spirit for me. These teachers fascinated me; they turned me on and around, confused my old self-image and what I had believed was real. The ones I remember had personal power; they were mystics, uncanny and impossible. I have experienced and loved other teachers, too, yet I seem to have forgotten them.

Though I never used the term "apprenticeship," I learned as if I were an apprentice. I studied with these teachers and was in therapy as much as possible—not only because I was neurotic, but because, above all, I found elements of shamanism in those relationships, in the love between master and apprentice. We focused on specific things, yet I studied the way they lived, basking in the incredible interactions they had with me and with others around them. They helped me to move my assemblage point and detach a bit from my phantom hood.

Healers and Teachers

I remember my first experience with the nagual in the person of Joan, a woman who suddenly appeared out of nowhere in the late 1960s. One day, while I was working in my little office on the lake of Zurich, the phone rang. I picked it up, and a voice on the other end said, "Hello, Dr. Mindell, this is Joan. Please don't hang up. I am calling you from the Zurich airport. Jesus, my spirit helper, told me to go to the airport in New York and wait for someone to give me the money to take a trip."

She explained that she had gone to Kennedy Airport and waited there for a few hours until someone actually gave her the money to buy a plane ticket. Her spirit had told her to buy a ticket to Zurich. Now she was standing in the Zurich airport, and Jesus had told her to open the phone book and call the first number her finger landed upon. That is why she was now on the telephone with me.

I was speechless, not just because I was in the middle of a session with a client, but because her story was so fantastic. I told her that I would make some time and would be waiting when she arrived. An hour later, she was sitting in my office, telling me that her spirit wanted me to start writing books. I protested that I was only twenty-eight and was just finishing my studies. I was convinced that I had nothing to say.

Joan ignored my protestations and simply told me that her spirit insisted that I write. I had never been interested in writing, but she proceeded to tell me that writing would heal my biggest problem. I laughed and told her that my biggest problem was my huge financial debt. She was silent and went into a trance. When she spoke a few minutes later, she ignored my problem and said that I should not pay so much attention to what my colleagues were doing but should get on with my own work. I loved what she was saying, but I doubted her. We decided to see each other several times more.

A breakthrough happened one morning when she came into my office and told me that her spirit had said I should stop playing with myself at night. I became furious and denied that I did that, even though I did. From then on, however, I took her spirit seriously.

After I had had about ten sittings with Joan, she left Zurich. Ten years later, my first book, *The Dreambody,* appeared, and soon thereafter other books her spirit had predicted emerged from my typewriter. Books earn little for me, but the connections they have created with people around the world have enriched me beyond my wildest hopes. In addition, Joan had said things to me that time in Zurich about my relationships with others that had seemed outrageous but that have proven true years later.

Twenty years after our last contact in Switzerland, Joan suddenly reappeared. This time she found me in the back woods in a cabin somewhere in the American Northwest. She knocked on the door and walked right in, saying she had found the cabin by following an eagle. She walked past me into the cabin, saw Amy, and embraced her, calling her by name without ever having met her. Then she sat down and promptly reported that she had seen me on the steps of a courthouse fighting for new forms of education. She has always been far ahead of me. Perhaps it will take another twenty years for me to realize that educational vision.

Joan's message to me was that there is more to life than who I thought I was. I was attracted, mystified, even enlightened by her. When she was around, I felt so much energy that I could have run for miles. I was always buzzing. We were some pair.

But things were not perfect between us. Like most therapists, I certainly needed a push. But perhaps, like some shamans, her talents lay in listening to the spirits and not in listening to people. It seemed to me that when I did not follow or comprehend her spirit's messages, she—not her spirit—tried to force me to obey. I was no angel; I was as stubborn as possible. I was too impressed by my personal history and needed someone who could turn me on to my own powers of transformation, to help me become a warrior. I needed someone to give my assemblage point a shove. But instead of changing, I was turned off by her pushiness and her lack of interest in my ordinary self.

The tougher she became, the less enchanted I was with her. She was the master of incredible powers, but, in spite of her connection to infinity, she seemed to me to be a victim to her own one way. Her insistence upon this one way of doing things made her ordinary for me. Like others off the path of heart, she was possessed by the very spirit that healed and offered insight to others. She was a winning warrior who was losing the battle with the devil's weed, a savior who may not have heard the spirit's message herself. I remembered don Juan's warnings that people become "phantoms" when they are hypnotized by common sense, by others' beliefs, or by the spirit itself.

Gurus

Swamiji, a guru in India, was more complete than Joan and the witch doctors in his verbal descriptions of magical happenings. He had many negative predictions about the future of our world and a lot of magic. Shiva, he said, was the world field. If Shiva went against you, you might still live, but if the guru went against you, nothing could save you. One of the ashram's posted signs said that the disciple should choose no other teacher.

These statements did not befriend Amy, who is wary of nondemocratic procedures. I understood the warnings philosophically as a voice of old India, reminding us that the facilitator is as important as the spirit. Still, I feared that the guru might be a phantom and not a real person.

When we landed in the ashram after hours of traveling, we went straight to the meditation hall. In spite of my spiritual aspirations, I fell asleep in a heap in one corner. Amy heard me snoring and called over to me to wake me up. The guru, it seems, had broken his traditional routine and was going to appear this afternoon, instead of waiting until the evening. I loved his unpredictable nature. It reminded me of don Juan, who said that the hunter catches his prey because he is not like it, not fixed by heavy, inflexible routines.

The guru came forth from his private chambers and had us called to his feet to speak with him. Later, two of his disciples said that he had spoken longer with us than he had with anyone else in the fifteen years in which they had known him. I was touched by his interest in us.

I told the guru about my need for renewal and courage in world work. He responded that service, not meditation, was the fastest way to illumination. Here was someone who lived in a state of meditative detachment from the world, but who recommended service to others. I instantly felt at home with his attitude.

But the guru's forcefulness made me uncomfortable. No one can know another human being, and yet I got the impression that he was neither detached nor growing. Was I simply a modern man expecting the impossible from this person whose life was based upon a three-thousand-year-old tradition? I tried to remain open-minded and remembered that modern India has deep connections with Austroasiatic and aboriginal times.[1] Still, though he was a fearless sorcerer and a courageous human being trying to fill the empty position of eldership in a world devoid of elders, he, too, was a phantom, a real person with the potential to grow to completion without identifying as such. Why should I have expected him to be different? When will I stop looking for teachers and either discover them in myself or in the community as a whole?

In any case, according to the guru's interpretation of ancient texts, only if someone like the guru is present can an individual or organization survive. The symbolic meaning of this statement is that, without a shaman facilitator, individual and group processes may not unravel constructively. Nowhere are there enough shamans with second attention to pick up double signals or practice controlled abandon. There are always too few people around who are sufficiently humble to help the rest of the people move in and out of spirits in a field. Thus, only if someone or some group behaves as a wise elder can you survive as an individual or organization.

Gurus try to awaken your spiritual potential, yet their personal behavior, under the guise of tradition, sometimes violates your trust. If a teacher takes herself too seriously, she becomes a phantom, telling others what to do. But perhaps just such phantom teachers are the best teachers, reminding us that the truth must be discovered again and again, every moment.

Kenyan Healers

The Kenyan healers whom I mentioned in chapter 12 had advantages over Joan and Swamiji. They lived in a community that believed in them and that had no written history to obey. Joan lived in the Western world. Everything that the Kenyan healers did was communal and interactive as well as full of the nagual. For example, one healer agreed to heal us only after having asked us if we wanted and were ready for her healing. She insisted upon nothing. Her detachment gave me hope that she was a true warrior and seer. I told in chapter 12 how this beautiful person chanted and hummed herself into an incredible trance while her husband and son played their musical instruments. Others were there, too, including apprentices who were learning the art of witch doctors. She said that her son was also considered a student. We were all learners together.

After some minutes, the woman and the apprentices had fallen in seizure to the ground. Yet our healer had come back to ordinary reality after a while and asked us again if we wanted to go further. Our translator explained that she was saying that Western medicine could not help us with what was bothering us. We needed special treatment. I was all ready to dive into the healing ceremony, and Amy, too, after a moment's hesitation, gave her assent.

This time, both the man and the woman began chanting and sent everyone present into a deep reverie. The woman went into another trance, and others in the room also fell into trances, yelling and rolling about. The scene reminded me of some of our own workshops on altered states and made me feel at home. I even thought that what I do with people might have originated here. It seems that living the dreamingbody is a unifying, cross-cultural experience through which you can understand and be understood by others.

Suddenly, the healer's husband and son had become alarmed as the woman reached the greatest depth of her trance. They started questioning her rapidly in Swahili, but she did not respond. Our translator told us that the shaman had gone too far in her trance and had lost contact with reality. Her husband and son had become frightened and intervened by playing romantic music to woo her back to this world.

We were astounded that, in that system, as in Yaqui shamanism, drowning in the nagual was considered incorrect. Confusing real people and invisible spirits was strictly forbidden. Here was someone we could trust. This woman dealt with spirits without wanting to get carried away by them. She could love people but separate them from the spirits in the air. She was a master of everyday life, yet could leave the world and go into trance states and later talk about them. For me, she was a true and eternal teacher and a real person.

In any case, she regained consciousness and related her visions to us. She had seen the evil ones who were bothering us and proceeded to describe our greatest problems back home. What to do now was the question. She again asked us if we wanted to go on. We eagerly agreed, figuring it was too late to turn back now. She questioned us about our problems in great detail and then decided to intervene on our behalf in the spirit world.

Now we were asked to wait outside the mud hut with the rest of her group while our healers created a decorative sand painting on the hut floor. They painted the image of the evil spirits they had seen in their visions. When they were finished, they invited us back in. They explained that the next step was to create a ceremony to reverse the evil effects that were making us sick. They had decided to paint a picture in the sand of what had been done to us and then to reverse it. Amy and I were directed to sit on one part of the sand painting, huddling together under one shawl. Our hosts began chanting, praying, and dancing. They prepared medicines and brought in a pair of live chickens. I remember whispering to Amy, "Hey, this is getting scary. Sitting on the sand painting is great, but do you think we'll have to swallow that medicine?"

Fear had become my barrier. But it was too late to become nervous about dysentery or malaria. One of the shamans spooned the medicine into his own mouth and then, before we could resist, with the same finger, spooned it into ours. Like children, we put it in our mouths but hesitated, and he said quickly, "Swallow it!"

Ugh! Medicine! I discovered that it tastes the same the world over. But the ceremony was just beginning. We were directed to walk meditatively back and forth over the human-like figure painted on the sand, in order to reverse the bad effects. The healers bathed the chickens in sacred water and then slapped our bodies with the living chicken wings. I knew that live chickens were essential in African ritual, but having a live chicken wiped over your head, back, and chest is an experience to remember.

Finally, after what seemed like hours, we were allowed to go home to an uneasy sleep. Miraculously, we felt well the next day, and we returned to the hut to get new medicine, which had been prepared during the night, in our absence. We took our prescriptions and sat quietly for whatever was going to happen next. To our surprise, the entire village came for a meal of grilled chicken—the same birds that had been used in the ritual the night before. The love and friendship of our African family showed through all of their interactions with us. Our healers treated us warmly and kindly, leaving their shamanic visages from the night before ingrained in our memories forever.

The whole experience moved me to tears. These healers were real people, not phantoms. They were true elders, the caretakers and leaders of their tribe. They gave any child who came by their hut a penny in order to honor the powers from which power and "medicine" came. For them the child was the spirit behind healing. Everyone there was poverty-stricken, but the spirit of the child was rich and central to the art. That culture encouraged everyone to live with the unknown within the context of the everyday world.

Our shamans in this community were wise people who mediated between people and spirits, working directly with the local psychic field. At the same time, they worked in town at menial tasks. Our interpreter informed us that we were the first non-Africans to see that ceremony. Only once before had these people worked with a white person.

Their work impressed us for many reasons. First, they continually asked us for our agreement about going further. Second, they felt that it was crucial not to identify with any reality, either the world of the spirits or that of ordinary people. Yet they greatly respected both.

In fact, our healers understood that they went off track when they identified their "clients" with the spirits that bothered them, as the woman apparently did in the midst of the ceremony. This particularly impressed me. Most of us forget that we are different than the moods that possess us, that our friends, too, are different than their troublesome spirits. This viewpoint is especially difficult to hold when you get hurt by others. Then you identify others solely by their actions, neglecting to consider that what hurts you about someone else's behavior is a spirit or mood that not only possesses that person, but is in the air. By forgetting this, you forget to honor both the spirits and the people.

I cannot remember ever having seen a Western therapist inadvertently identify a client with her unconscious problem and then get out of that frame of mind. Jung apparently apologized if he got into bad moods with people. I also remember seeing other witch doctors do that. I recall how a Native American medicine healer living with a tribe in Canada lost his temper at Americans because of the way the Canadian government was treating Indians. He stormed out of the room in which we were doing a group process. Then he came back to apologize for his bad mood. Naturally, like most readers, I thought his anger was justified, but he felt it had harmed others, and he was genuinely apologetic. Here was another real teacher.

I don't want to place these wonderful people on pedestals too high, yet it was touching to see this man and our Kenyan healers take responsibility for their moods and their possible effects on the world around them. I have never seen anyone else consider what their moods do to the community they live in, much less apologize for these moods and change them. It is as if these healers were differentiating themselves from the spirits that moved them. I feel loved and privileged to be around others who worry not only about themselves but about what they are doing to me. Such human beings need to be honored.

These teachers gave me a lot. They awakened me to the spirit of large-group situations. In large gatherings and in general, your viewpoint only partially belongs to you. A viewpoint is also a spirit in the field, which, taken together with all the other spirits, makes the world whole. My definition of being a real person is being awake to the spirits that go through you and taking responsibility for their effects on others.

Whenever you get stuck, you are momentarily possessed by the spirit of a role that you are inadvertently playing. The healing for this situation is, as our healers showed us, intervening between the people and the spirits and encouraging the people to express the spirits and move on. If you are attracted by one and the same spirit or role all the time, you are unfree. Still, you are only the channel and not the spirit itself. If you choose to forget this, you become a phantom instead of a real person.

In central Africa, where Western psychotherapy has had little impact, shamanic methods are used when Western medicine fails. The shamanic approach does not require anything more from the "client" than he can give. The shamans are compassionate with the suffering, phantomlike nature of the clients and do not blame the clients for being as they are. These shamans try not to become phantoms themselves.

The shamans who healed us took full responsibility for their awareness of the spirit and only asked for minimal commitment for their awareness. No integration was required— except, of course, for the taking of the medicine. Shamanic healing works with anyone, even with those not overtly interested in becoming warriors. We wanted to pay these people, but before they would take anything from us, they had to go into trance to feel what was right for the spirit. What healed most of all was that these shamans were real people.

Phantoms and Real People

The phantom, unlike the warrior, ignores ghosts and simply becomes possessed by them. For the phantom, everything is terribly serious. When you are a phantom, you are constantly in pain, troubled, worried about the state of the world, caught up in either destroying or saving it.

How do you become a real person instead of a phantom? As I wrote in chapter 6, whether you become a hunter or a warrior is a matter of the spirit. At every stage of development, personal growth is a matter of an unknown force. You remain a phantom, or you may for moments become a hunter. Then you track your prey, kill it, and eat or integrate it while remaining in ordinary reality. Perhaps you become a warrior. Then you confront the other world and step into it.

The person on the path of heart, however, is everything and nothing. In this state, you are a real person, almost detached, moving fluidly and rapidly between states. Sometimes you are just an ordinary person, sometimes a warrior, sometimes a nagual teacher.

There are times when you must coerce yourself and make a vow to step out of the morass of the self-importance and moods of phantom life. You may need to vow never to lose another battle with the ally and to forget your whole self. This vow always seems to come after you have had enough of your own moods, boredom, and compulsions. A growing need arises—after you have been drugged enough by moody, foggy conditions—to become the one who processes these states instead of the one who is depressed or inflated.

But if the vow fails, you must wait for a signal from the unknown. What else can upset the phantom's belief that the world is a place in which to succeed and fail instead of a hunting ground in which to be transformed? The phantom's viewpoint is everyone's reality. When you are a phantom, either you are bored with life, because you have no goal, or you swing wildly between enthusiasm and depression, depending on whether you have done something.

As a real person on the path of heart, you may appear to be like everyone else: stubborn and ambitious, jealous and insulted. But your laughter gives you away. There is something free about you in this state. You practice democracy at the deepest level, listen to inner and outer voices, and live and leave each voice as the moment requires.

Ancient and modern shamans follow their dreams and wait for magic animals and unpredictable turns of fate to gain access to this appealing state of mind. They wait for their calling. Today, however, the very time of day may be the calling. By the virtue of your being alive today, you are called upon to develop your potential for the second attention and controlled abandon or to admit that you take no responsibility for the environment.

Now is the time to do business by dreaming with others together. If you are viewed as weird or fantastic today, you may console yourself. Tomorrow, phantomhood, which ignores the spirit and is possessed by it, will be seen as an epidemic disease with a high mortality rate.

EXERCISES

1. Describe yourself when you are a phantom. Which moods tend to possess you longest, and what do you look like when you are possessed? Notice what feeling like a phantom does to your body. Notice when and if your phantomlike moods serve or provoke the enlightenment or development of others.

2. Describe yourself when you are real. Notice what you look and feel like when you feel fluid and can act like a phantom and also detach from it. In these real moments, what role do you fill in the world around you? When you are real, perhaps you feel as if you are on the path of heart. Others around you may need you in this role; they may even participate in creating the role for you to occupy.

3. Honor your teachers. Which men and women in your past have played the role of the spirit for you, of your nagual? Who confused your old worldview and helped you to become real? Remember your favorite teachers. What were their tasks in life? How far did they get with their tasks? How are you in the midst of completing their tasks? Choose one teacher now to honor, and take a moment with the following fantasy. Think of this person as part of a line of real people. Imagine what spirit or what mythical or real teachers were behind that person.

4. Now look back into history and see your real teachers and the spirit lineage standing behind them. This vision may connect you not only to your teacher, but to yourself, as a real person with an incredible history. Take a moment and experiment with honoring your teacher, your lineage, and even yourself.

CHAPTER 14

THE DEATHWALK

I f you wrestle your demon, you find moments of pleasure, freedom, and exceptional energy— whether you win or lose the battle with yourself. Perhaps best of all, you have moments of feeling real and congruent, free from the fears and symptoms of phantomhood. Now you know you have a double and sense your shaman's dreamingbody. But sometimes you forget these experiences and wonder just how much of the dreamingbody can be lived in this life. On the one hand, your love for the world tempts you back to pester and play with everyone else. But on the other hand, the ecstasy of experience may entice you to leave forever.

In the last pages of *Tales of Power*, don Juan explains to his apprentice that the place in which they stand is their last crossroads together. Few warriors, he says, have ever survived the encounter with the unknown, which the apprentices are about to face. The nagual is so intense that those who go through the final encounter find it unappealing to return to the tonal, "the world of order and noise and pain."[1]

Remember those dramatic feelings of wholeness that accompany the discovery of the dreamingbody? It is difficult to leave such an experience and go back to ordinary reality. Returning from a wonderful vacation, a meaningful relationship, or an intense inner experience is painful, because you fear losing the connection to your whole self.

Thus, you experience difficulties after your encounter with the nagual. Returning to the state of ordinary affairs— the world of the tonal, where dreams, body experiences, and secondary processes are not valued—is not easy. Don Juan warns his apprentice that if he does not choose to return, he will disappear, as if swallowed by the earth. But if he does return, he will have to wait and finish his particular task in life. Once this is finished, the apprentice will have command over the totality of himself. If he returns, don Juan explains, he will be confronted for the first time with the idea of the task to be fulfilled. This is no ordinary job, don Juan warns, but a worldly undertaking that may take a long time to complete. The task the apprentice must fulfill is one bestowed upon him by his teacher.

Don Juan tells Castaneda that in earlier times, teachers never searched for apprentices. The personal power of both teacher and apprentice set up their relationship, so that force, desire, or intrigue never bonded the two. Since power chooses the teacher, you may also assume that power chooses the task linked to that particular teacher.

I can verify this from personal experience. When I first went to Zurich, my intention was to complete my studies in theoretical physics. Fate had it, however, that I stumbled into a fellow student who was so infatuated with his analyst that I decided to enter analysis as well. Thus, fate introduced me to my first teacher.

Then one day, while I was sitting outside a cafe watching the people go by, I noticed a charming European gentleman sitting at the next table doing the same thing. As I looked at him closely, I saw in him a mixture of old-world-style and wakeful presence. I asked him what he was doing, and he replied dryly, "Same thing as you."

We spent an enjoyable afternoon together, talking about women and cafes, and decided to meet again the next Saturday afternoon. The next week we had a wonderful time again, and we continued to meet each Saturday afternoon, until one day I dreamed that this man was my real teacher. At the time of my dream, many weeks after we had first met, we had been so busy chatting, drinking, and laughing that we had not yet introduced ourselves. What was his name?

The next time I saw him, I shyly told him my dream and asked him if he were also interested in dreams and such things. He laughed aloud and said yes, he had recently gotten interested in such things. He must have seen how puzzled I was by his behavior, for he looked me straight in the eye and told me that he was president of the Jung Institute in Zurich, and the nephew of C. G. Jung. Shocked, the official aspect of my apprenticeship began.

We spent a lot of time together, and he became a true and incomprehensible nagual for me. He was at once a spiritual teacher and a man thoroughly anchored in this world. He told me his job was to teach me about the unconscious through living; we spent most of our time together doing anything but conventional analysis. We walked, talked, and met at unusual times and in strange places. Later on, we met with others; I loved watching him interact with others. He was so charming, and I felt so antisocial. Today, I realize how lucky I was to have met him.

Inevitably, my task became wrapped up with this man's fate, and when he died years after our first meeting, I dreamed on the day of his funeral that his double jumped out of the grave and into my lungs when I inhaled. Sometimes I still feel that a part of him is in me, which may be why he still appears in my dreams, directing me about the nature of my personal task.

Since that time, a few people have chosen me to be their teacher, and I have been amazed at how clearly the dreams of these people link their tasks to mine. The personal powers of both the teacher and the student set up their meeting, and the same power chooses the task symbolized by that teacher. In other words, the task is a shared spirit, which in some cases may take generations to complete. It is as if student and teacher are part of a long lineage whose history and future extend backward and outward to infinity.

There is something freeing about the antiquity and impersonality of the task, and something wonderful about the participation of those who are living and dead in fulfilling it. Relationships at this level are both intimate and free. I remember learning this from a man in Bombay who came to me after seeing me for the first time at a lecture. He said, "Dr. Mindell, I would like you to be my guru." I recoiled a bit, feeling embarrassed, and began wondering how to deal with his feelings.

Today I am grateful to him, however, for having been a guru for me in showing me how to deal with feelings. "Dr. Mindell, don't worry about this. It is impersonal," he explained. "It has nothing to do with you and me. You have become my guru, but you do not have to do anything. I will carry your picture with me and talk to it when necessary."

Though this may sound to a Westerner like a one-sided attitude, there is eternal truth to it. The apprentice's and teacher's powers create their relationship and their task. All connected to the myth of consciousness have at least one task in common: to develop the second attention and relativize the one-sidedness of our awareness, enabling ourselves and others to live more fully. Castaneda's task, for example, was apparently to bring the powers of the night into the day via the teachings of don Juan.

The exact nature of the task depends upon your individual talents and weaknesses, the period you live in, and the aspect of your teacher's task that she has not completed. Hence, it is just as don Juan says: The task is bestowed by the spirit of the teacher, either directly or indirectly through dreams and love.

Deathwalk

Don Genaro tells about problems connected with this task. He recounts a tale of what happens while you wait for the task to be completed, a time that I call the deathwalk. According to this story, there was a band of male warriors who lived in the mountains many years ago. When one member of the band disobeyed the group rules, he had to face the others and explain himself to them. They found him either innocent or guilty; if they found him guilty, they lined up to shoot him while he walked in front of them.

The condemned warrior, however, was given a chance. If he walked in such a special way that no one could pull the trigger, or if he survived his wounds, he was free. The story goes that in fact some people did manage to live through that deathwalk. Perhaps their personal power touched their comrades, making it impossible for the others to shoot. Or perhaps the condemned warrior was so centered and calm that his detachment saved him.

According to the shamans, this story means that if you choose to return to everyday life after your training, you must wait on this earth until your task is done. Your waiting will be like that walk of the warriors in the story: Every step could be your last. The difference is that your comrades are the executioners in the story, whereas in real life, the spirit itself is aiming at you.[2]

In any case, everyone caught in this situation has "run out of human time," and the only things that can save you will be your learning and the impeccability you employ while completing your task. This means that you are on a deathwalk. Your interest in awareness and personal growth binds you with others, not only through mutual friendship, but through your need for challenge and provocation.

Conflict, both inner and outer, is the fate of the warrior. All are in the midst of a deathwalk insofar as the world constantly challenges you to become your entire self. An average person feels that the world is against her. The difference between the state of mind of an ordinary person and that of a warrior is that a warrior realizes that the worst conflict is with his own phantom nature. As a warrior, you know that the world is a hunting ground, and everyone is an ally, tripping and troubling you until you tap the ally's power, the dreamingbody.

Thus, your warrior's death squad is composed of both your inner critics and outer friends and enemies—depending upon your state of mind. Friends can be worthy opponents, demons, and allies, whose secrets you must discover. They seem like opposing powers within you and all around the universe. These erstwhile friends are your mythic warrior group, inner and outer criticism, generated by jealousy and unconsciousness, by your relationship to a teacher and to fellow students, and by your own ally, which breaks social rules. This group is dreaming together.

The Rules

The implicit laws of this inner or outer group are the rules of your community, the intentions you have somehow agreed to live by. They may be the unwritten laws of your family and culture and/or the ideals and rationale of the nation. Within your warrior's family, they are that group's laws governing relationships and the roles of women and men. They are the implicit rules of dealing with outsiders. If you are part of a religious group, you live by certain rules that govern belief and lifestyle. If you are a scientist, you are bound by the conventions of empiricism and rationalism. As a teacher, you must model academic behavior and teach people to adapt. For the therapist, rationalism is supposed to win over shamanism.

As a person, you must follow the definitions of normal human behavior and repress perceptions that lie outside this definition. Your racial group frowns upon mixed relationships. As a woman, you must fight three thousand years of domination. As a man, you must work until you drop—no relaxing! If you are gay, lesbian, or bisexual, you must be careful about showing that, or you could be killed.

If your particular group attacks you first in your dreams, then you can go into therapy and meet your own resistances. Yet this may not succeed, because self-doubt, that is, your attackers, can block you even from seeking help, dreaming, or moving. Inner attacks are at their maximum when you attempt to change and be real. Sometimes only a shaman who looks for your lost soul can help.

The jury spirit manifests outwardly as your neighbor, a group, a country, the tax department, the world. In fact, your very existence on the planet at the turn of the twenty-first century means that you are bound by the conventions of the past and the hope of a new age. At any time, you are requested from inside and out to do as others do and to identify with what others want you to be. Changing without permission is forbidden.

The world of your attackers is like a gigantic phantom field in which you must move. As you work and fulfill your task, you become fluid, changing from moment to moment, coming from and returning to old roles, inadvertently breaking the central rule: Do not tamper with your own personal history. But, of course, you have had to.

Upsetting your own sense of yourself, changing identities, and dropping personal history has been tough and exciting. Now it is shocking to hear old friends accusing you of breaking the explicit and implicit rules of the past. This conflict is painful enough, but worse is to come. Breaking a group rule puts you against a far more formidable foe than even intimate family and friends. The rule breaker must stand before centuries of human assumptions and the outrage of its defenders.

Fate has made you an outlaw. As a warrior, you one day had to disobey one of these cultural laws, almost by definition. You upset and threatened belief systems and goals. Since you are a warrior, you have had to step over edges and unwittingly disturb the web of which you are part. Your body stops the world by living the energy in symptoms. Awareness and the second attention make you more unpredictable in relationships. Your sense of the unknown leads you to support spirits that others have forgotten. Now you are in trouble.

The Executioners

Is it your fault if you remind others of dreams they do not want? And who can blame the group, either for resistance to you or for the life-and-death struggle that ensues? These people are fighting for their lives, equilibrium, homeostasis—indeed, for the perpetuation of history. "Do not disturb us more than we can take," they say.

From a global viewpoint, you disturb your organizational system, and history must fight for continuity. In this universal and fated interaction, the warrior's friends become the voices of the web. Their warmth turns to ice. They accuse you of unjustifiable behavior, egotism, and criminality as they become possessed by their lawmaker role in this eternal drama of human history.

The collective you live in must pursue you for what it experiences as criminal acts and bring you to trial, just as you have challenged other rule breakers in the past. Now it is you who enters into a life-and-death struggle with the universe. It is your warrior's fate to feel prosecuted and to face the collective jury. The ecstasy of the nagual suddenly turns into a nightmare as your closest friends become your worthy opponents, challenging you to take responsibility for your acts.

If you are not careful, you fall back into phantomhood and strike back at those who injure you. With luck and awareness, however, you remember the warrior's view and realize the significance of your battle. Your comrades are not simply the lowly phantoms you once despised, and their shots are not the attacks that make you bleed. Rather, they are the voice of history asking you to repay culture by expanding your sense of yourself to include others. Either remove yourself from your acts and see your trouble as a debt you owe history, or fight like a hero and die like a phantom.

The beginning warrior forgets these grand visions in the midst of her tensions and in the crucial moment claims before the court that she had no choice, that she had to commit her crime. If you had not heeded the words of the demon, expressed the impulsiveness of your dreamingbody, and obeyed the commands of her death, you would have become sick and disordered. You could not have said yes once again to the demands of adaptation and no to your inner world. There was no middle way of reasonableness.

Though their hearts may be stirred, the jury's verdict must still be "guilty." Following inner life and producing trouble are not allowed. Either follow the ally by yourself, they will say, or follow the rules of the collective. To follow the ally within the collective is to disturb others.

This jury may complain that as long as you are around, business can no longer go on as usual. Why must you go in the opposite direction? Wouldn't it be easier to follow the prescribed routes that others seem to walk? How can you smile at things others take so seriously and be serious about what others ignore? The jury would like to give you another chance—indeed, you may be a remarkable person—but it cannot do so because your nature won't allow it to. These people must shoot to kill you at the edge of the cliff and make certain that you realize that your acts were a matter of life and death.

Thus, your lesson is that following the ally secures neither collective approval nor longevity. The path of knowledge is a forced one in which you constantly meet inexplicable powers. The path of heart is as terrifying as it is meaningful. It could result in early death.

According to don Genaro and don Juan, some warriors have been so centered that they have made it across the firing range without being shot. Their comrades just could not pull the trigger. Was the warrior so congruent and at one with his previous acts and crimes that his dreamingbody pulled him through unharmed? Or was he just so tough that he recuperated from a broken heart and wounds?

Perhaps it was not the warrior who governed the situation but the members of his jury who realized that their friend was living something out for everyone. After all, every band of warriors, every group of people, is connected by some sort of awareness myth. Each part of the group is a channel of awareness capable of carrying and expressing messages from the unknown.

An enlightened jury would have to reason that if the town kills one of its citizens, it only succeeds in destroying his body. The voice and message carried by that warrior cannot be killed. New ideas and ways of living are more vast and more permanent than the people who speak them. The ideas will haunt the town in its dreams long after the warrior has died. In this way, the voices of the past continue today as roles in the present, parts that are needed for the sake of collective wholeness. This is why witchcraft, shamanism, and, I hope, indigenous life can never be completely destroyed.

In any case, since you are a temporary rule breaker within the group, you are also its secondary process, its ghost spirit. To kill you is not only inhuman, but ineffectual. Dreams live on after your death. No idea has ever been killed. Besides, you might argue, your community's rulership could have been too rigid; otherwise, it would not have dreamed up a warrior to unwittingly create a revolution.

If you face the jury today, you will have the feeling that you have been here before. The global viewpoint that you are everyone who has ever broken a rule may enable you to survive. The jury, which fights for the ways things have been, has also always been here. Moreover, not only you are on trial, but so is all of humanity that has broken environmental rules.

You are living in a world that itself is on trial. So remind your potential executioners that they, too, have run out of time. As human beings thrash about for solutions to the overwhelming and apparently unsolvable planetary problems they have created, nature is aiming at the human species, just as the jury aims at the warrior.

Yet you know that you cannot wait for your world to awaken spontaneously, for you may observe its change from the grave. You must wake up and can no longer afford to see your rule breaker's journey as only a personal battle of individuation. The results of your deathwalk are important for everyone. Your individual attempts to become your whole self are provoking change around you, even now as you read this. Eternity asks you, so to speak, to model world change as the whole planet considers how it will survive its deathwalk with nature.

To survive the deathwalk, you must be both vulnerable and invisible. First you must cry for yourself, as the victim of your own and other's unconsciousness. Then you must stand strongly and congruently for yourself, against opponents. Finally, you must drop your personal history and smile. If you have gotten this far, you have the power even to take sides with your jury, to see its viewpoint and attack yourself before it can shoot. Now, if you succeed at nothing else, at least you will be on the path of heart and learning.

Remember death, your old adviser? Disappear before the guns of the enemy and remove your own personal history before it can shoot. As a fluid warrior, not only are you yourself, but you have the opinions of the jury. Moreover, you are a spirit or a role in a field. Your fluidity should give you compassion both for yourself and for your persecutors, friends, and community. The moment you find your shaman's body, you will gladly admit that your time is up. The jury that witnesses such a last stand, in which you leave your own history, will be a jury that has had its job taken away.

Such a last dance may not uphold death, but it will surely preserve you forever. Like a spirit free from all roles, the legendary warrior carries her body and her death in her own hands and sees her life in perspective. The world is not only her enemy but her awakener. Something eternal watches the way she deals with minority opinions. Something huge is sensitive to unconsciousness and brutality.

The worst problem with the deathwalk is not its inevitability or even its universality, but the way you and everyone else freeze into a particular role during its occurrence, afraid to move or to admit that everyone is on trial. We are all gods who could facilitate pain but usually don't. Thus, each time one of us takes the witness stand, the whole world goes on trial. Every time a disturber tests the rules, the entire group is under examination.

History reminds us that a few have always survived and transformed together with their communities. There has always been a don Juan who has taught about the totality of human beings, who has gone on the path of self-discovery, returned to Ixtlan, and gone on to transform others. In fact, our present study is due to don Juan's own survival of the deathwalk. He must have been impossible for those around him, but he lived through their anger and loved them enough to give as much as he took.

Until now, our world has gone through a relentless cycle of dreaming up and killing its most unusual shamans and teachers, who have then returned in other forms to help. There has always been a Lao Tsu, returning in the last moment before death to write a *Tao Te Ching*. Think of the Native American chief Hiawatha and his dreams, which helped him teach his group how to plant new crops and survive. Or consider the dramatic story of the Swiss Bruder Klaus, who left his family at age forty-five in order to follow his Wotanic dreams and later repaid the world with political and divine guidance.[3] Remember Jesus, Buddha, Gandhi, Martin Luther King, Jr., and Malcolm X. Remember Ben Thompson, the man who read this chapter on tape and had it played back at his funeral.

I recall many unsung grassroots heroes who have passed their lives in relative obscurity, suffering the antithetical nature of their path with the world around them. Their allies have appeared as physical or social disabilities, homosexuality, color differences, forbidden loves, madness, and poetry. I think of single parents and of lonely artists trying to express the impossible. And others have lived their fates through to the moment of death without the support of anyone besides their own dreaming process.

Understanding that the world dreamed their unconventionality into existence would have been a small comfort for the heartache left over when the battle was finished. But what would really honor the memory of these people would be our realization that those small changes that occurred because of their struggle touch everyone today, because they are present everywhere, at all times, in the network of connections.

The Length of Life

Thus nation and community determine in part the length of an individual's life. In fact, the average age of human beings must be connected to the way in which you destroy or support others. The length of your life may be set by more than genetic inheritance, good food, physical exercise, and good and bad deeds. Just as biologists cannot properly explain the pulse of life or the moment of death, no one knows why an individual will live eighty years and not one hundred or five hundred. No one knows why so many talented, gifted, and incredible people die early.

I never thought about this problem until I read this chapter as if I were Ben Thompson speaking at my funeral. I think Ben was trying to say that his life had been a deathwalk, which ended, like all our lives will, at the point where the message he carried was too early for its time.

Perhaps you die when you fail to communicate or when others cannot understand the messages of the spirit within you. You die every time you fail to appreciate the oppressor who has forced you to define your true nature. Instead of being annihilated, as if by evil, you can still drop your personal history, become a fluid piece of antimatter, step out of time, and become your double, your opponent.

Until now, too few of us have followed nature's mysteries, the messages and signals of the unknown. Taking responsibility for the ruthlessness of life means having the courage to focus upon processes that others neglect. The same relentlessness that possesses you could be the ally, which, once transformed, will nourish. Then your deathwalk will not only be your personal difficulties but the dramatic tale of global awakening.

EXERCISES

1. Recall some of the deathwalks you are on or have been on. When you were a child, did you battle with other children? As a teenager, did you have trouble with authorities? Did you run into conflict with your immediate family? Have you been involved in forbidden love affairs? Have you had or are you in an unconventional partnership or marriage? Have you experienced a midlife crisis, in which everything became meaningless? Are you afraid of illness, retirement, old age, or death? Are you about to do something that will bring you into conflict with others?

2. Imagine an opponent or jury that is now or might in the future be against you. Who is it? What does it look like? What is it doing and saying? Where is it?

3. Choose one of these encounters that you would like to complete now. Encounter your inner or outer opponents,

at first in your mind's eye. Notice what they are doing, thinking, feeling.

4. Get into your double. Pick up your double signals in your imagination, and watch how your shaman's body deals with the situation.

5. If you need to, remind your attackers that we are all on a deathwalk and that nature is aiming at the entire human race, judging the way in which we all handle conflict. Tell your attackers that eternity might put them on trial, too, for their abusiveness.

6. If you have sufficient perspective, refer to history. Tell the inner or outer opponents that you are a part of culture that has been neglected. Tell them that others have tried and failed at this deathwalk or have not had the courage to begin. Explain ways in which the future might be better for all if the jury tried to understand your actions.

7. Listen to your opponents, and notice what strong, nonverbal body feelings occur. If you cannot defend yourself or speak, let your feelings express themselves in movement. Allow this moment to be your last dance, and allow your dance to unfold.

CHAPTER 15

DREAMTIME AND CULTURAL CHANGE

Remember the pain of the deathwalk. Remember what it was like when others treated you as an unwanted dream. When you survive a deathwalk, you know what it is like for a dream to almost die, for a community to turn against you, for an ethnic group to be tortured. If you do not recognize your own powers, when the country represses the diversity of its citizens, its people use guns in order to dream together.

There are only slight differences in the pain caused by unnecessary self-criticism, contempt from a family, oppression by a group, or scorn because you have followed your shaman's body. But if you survive the deathwalk, you could help transform our present epidemic of abuse, oppression, and genocide into a state of people dreaming together.

To do this, notice abuse when it occurs. Notice racism, homophobia, religious prejudice, and sexism. Point out to everyone how we force individuals to enter into a deathwalk as they go down the street, live at home, or stand in public. Bring forward the deadly spirits, like the oppressor, and encourage everyone to witness the agony of the victim. In chapter 12, I gave examples of racism and anti-Semitism and indicated how to encourage confrontation between the various spirits and people.

When we succeed at dreaming together, everyone realizes that we are all responsible for creating and changing culture. It is everyone's job to witness and investigate the altered states of oppression, pain, rage, and freedom that permeate our groups. We have not alleviated our cultural problems by repressing, avoiding, or ignoring them. We need new shamans to go deeper into them. Dreaming together is a new kind of social activism; it means going deeper to find the basis of personal and social healing.

When you succeed at mixing innerwork and group process, no one carries grudges or sees the events that have occurred as only personal. In dreaming together, everyone knows that not only the resolution to conflict is crucial, but so is the sense of common participation in awesome events.

Most cultures have forgotten their indigenous origins. The modern world looks to me like a ship lost at sea, a ship searching for its past. As it flounders about, it tries in vain to anchor itself on fundamentalism, heroic leadership, dictatorship, or war, those ancient mirages of meaning. Everyone seems to have forgotten the meaning that personal lives have in the evolution of communities. Yet as our planet searches for new paradigms of democracy, the central myth of community—dreaming together, the power that once created the world—lies only one breath away.

Remaining aboriginal cultures still teach about dream-time. Native American stories recall how one man's dream changed the entire tribe. One such story, of Black Elk,[1] tells about how a whole tribe dreamed together.

I awoke to the importance of dreaming together after being with Australian aborigines. The healer Amy and I visited in the darkness of the South Pacific bush, that down under world, greeted us quietly in the evening shadows one night and asked us to come again, to meet him the next day. He needed time to search the rainforest for healing plants.

While going home that night, we were driving through the healer's village when a man who seemed to be wandering aimlessly almost walked in front of our car. We stopped, and I opened the door to say hello. The aboriginal man got in, right next to me, without a word. This wonderful being asked to be taken home. At first he seemed intoxicated to the point of delirium, but after a few minutes of complete trancelike behavior, he spoke clearly about himself. He was living somewhere between the oppression of colonial Australia, which refused to accept aborigines as human beings until only a few years ago, and the nonviolent dreamtime of the aborigines. When he finally introduced us to his family at his home, we experienced that same warmth, friendship, and love that we had missed since we left Mombasa.

If you look down on aboriginal cultures for their drinking problems, then consider the possibility that alcohol is a way back to dreamtime. Modern culture divides us from our ancient myths of a planet created by dreamlike figures who come out at night. According to these myths, the world was not created by the big bang and its resulting geophysical forces. The world is the way it is because of the mythic Australian red kangaroo and other deities.[2] Whenever you imagine the environment full of spirits, you connect to the most ancient part of human history, which dates back fifty thousand years. Just as you may experience dragons and people within you, your aboriginal mind sees the world as the expression of mythic powers that curve the space and time of geology.

The day after we met that aboriginal man, we returned to the Australian healer, who invited us, one at a time, into his hut to be healed. In the seance done for me, the healer and his wife chanted and danced. She sang, while he rubbed his hands, first on his own body and then on mine to heal me. The couple listened closely to the problems I described and finally blew the soul back into me through my ears and the top of my head. He "brushed me clean" by waving a medicine plant over my body. Later, gathering us together, he "smoked us pure" by asking us to stand in front of his fire, where the fumes of burning healing plants were blown through us by the wind.

It was an awesome and difficult-to-describe affair. The couple's daughter sat patiently outside the hut and waited to tell us that we should not discuss our experiences with anyone. However, she said, I could later write about these experiences in this book.

I understand traditional secrecy. Wherever some form of dreamtime appears, something mysterious happens that is so individual it may be incomprehensible to anyone in a normal state of consciousness. It is dangerous to talk about such things, not only because you can hurt the healing spirits, but because your sense of the uncanny is so fragile. Every time you experience an amazing event, your shaman's body goes on a deathwalk before all your conventional spirits. Your rational brothers and sisters, who are also possessed by the "doings" of the times, oppose or feel endangered by such experiences.

Although healers may use the same methods on many different people, their powers can cause you to have utterly individual and singular experiences that cannot be duplicated. Every moment with such people is dreaming together, and your moment of power.

After the "smoking," we stood around the fire until dusk and chatted with the healer's extended family, who had gathered for our ceremony. That night, I dreamed that we were in the high Himalayas. This "peak" experience was finding a community whose fifty-thousand-year history supported dreaming together. The couple's daughter told me it was OK to write about this experience, perhaps because dreaming together is everyone's chance for a peak experience, a cultural renewal.

Community and Relationship

According to both our African and our Australian shamans, illness could be caused by the jealousy of others. People could spook or poison you directly, or they could hire someone else to do so. The healers did not deny that you could also get sick from something more mundane, even from "too much worry or rush." But the big problems, they say, are connected to jealousy.

What I call networking, the aboriginal healer called dreaming. Community consists not only of people speaking together but of the web of people, trees, and spirits that dream together. Dreaming is a type of force and can have serious consequences, for it permeates all of life. If you live in a Western-style city and have relationship problems, you probably work on yourself or try to work out your problems with others involved. But indigenous healers have other ideas. They say you suffer from the power of bad spirits, from jealous demons that are after you. The worst magic is voodoo, an intervention that comes from the jealousy of others and is meant to injure you.

Our healers had nothing to say about talking directly to those who were jealous of us but were clear about the lethal consequences unleashed through their bad feelings. You may think aboriginal relationship beliefs treat jealousy too seriously. But consider the following. If someone looks at you in a nasty way, you feel uncomfortable. If several people in a room are in conflict, the atmosphere becomes unbearable. Thoughts have power, and negative thoughts injure. That is why indigenous peoples say that we live in a magical dreamtime, a global dreamfield where parapsychological synchronicities and illness from jealousy can occur.

Since we are interconnected, you, as a warrior, must watch carefully over your feelings for yourself, for others, and for the environment. Because the trees and plants are your relatives, according to the earliest beliefs, the feelings you have about them can make them live or die. Indigenous peoples have developed customs in which kindness is important, not only because people are good-hearted. As an aboriginal person, you learn not only to respect yourself and others, but to honor nature if you want to survive in the environment. You are taught to treat nature as an equal, a relative, a parent, a brother, or a sister; otherwise, you injure the world by forgetting that it, too, can dream. Not only is whatever you feel your business, it is a political reality, a dreambody experience that you feel in your gut, that the trees notice in their leaves and roots, that even rocks sense. Without respect for nature, neither modern medicine nor green politics can save your body or the trees.

The priestesses of the oldest shamanistic religions—in South, Central, and North America; Oceania; Australia; Tibet; China; Europe; and the Far East—begin with going into a trance and dreaming something with someone. Dreaming together is like the quantum reality with which physicists work; it occurs in a field waiting for actuality through your participation and observation, through your active dreaming. Wherever you move on this earth, you move with me and others through this field, our common home. Whatever you dream is part of our dreaming together.

You can kill aboriginal people, but you cannot kill dreamtime. In a way, shamanism can never die out. Today, people go to discos and dance themselves into a trance, not only because they need exercise and want entertainment. They are trying to dream together. You watch football games to see the accidental mixed with the impeccable, to dream with thousands of others. When you meet with other people and dreaming does not happen, you get bored and avoid such meetings in the future. You smoke and drink to dream. You take drugs or overeat. You probably even go to restaurants to dream with others. You put on your costume, your nicest clothes, to leave one part and become another part of yourself, to dream with others, even though you may not have identified socially accepted altered states of consciousness (like changing costumes) as a form of dreaming together.

Psychologists identify basic human drives such as sex, death, love, power, and the hope for transcendence. I add another drive to this list: that of dreaming together. This is the community's way of following the Tao by following secondary processes. It is the aboriginal way. In the West, you may feel successful if you are famous, rich, or good-looking. But aboriginal people do not feel completely successful until their relationships are in order, until their community is well. Success in the indigenous sense depends in part upon dreaming together. In a world so full of trouble, dreamtime is the only place where it is both unsafe and safe. All want to participate in creating the world, to find awesome powers and also community.

Creating peace in the world, preserving our environment, caring for one another, protecting our most basic human right—the right to live—all cannot be accomplished without new cultures able to work on the emotional problems not touched by political dialogue. We must learn to get along with our neighbors. Yet, until now, we have only focused upon negotiations between people in conflict who are willing to talk with one another. We avoid psychological and emotional problems. This is equivalent to focusing only upon politicians interested in popularity and not upon people who must die in battle. We cannot continue with such oversight if we intend to live in a more peaceful world.

I recall a conference in Russia in 1993 on conflict resolution. Members of the parliaments and delegations from groups in conflict from various regions of the ex-Soviet Republic attended. After I asked that the government people and peace activists from Georgia, Azerbaijan, Armenia, Abkhazia, Ossetia, and Ingushetia stand in a circle together, someone from Georgia broke the silence by saying that this was the first time in history that these groups had even agreed to be in the same room. I went further and recommended sitting on the floor. Again, there was dead silence as representatives of these groups sat together in a circle. Slowly, one after another, these men and women spoke of the suffering of their people, describing war, poverty, and ongoing racial prejudice.

Amy and I listened carefully and noticed that several spirits were mentioned but not visible. People spoke of terrorists invading their localities; others mentioned the effects of imperialist policies of the ex-Soviet leaders in Moscow, but I could find neither an imperialist nor a terrorist in the room.

I explained that, even though we had been employed by the ex-Soviet Peace Committee to work on these conflicts, imperialism and terrorism were unrepresented spirits in our present community of nations. Since negotiations on the political level were failing, why not dream together? To my immense surprise, I was immediately understood. People got up to play and stood in places set aside for the three spirits: the imperialist, the terrorist, and the victimized community. A dramatic tension had filled the room, when suddenly everything exploded into roars of laughter. I almost fell over backward in shock when these dignified women and men transformed into spirits. Some stepped into Moscow's role of imperialists and demanded that everyone submit to their domination. The terrorists screamed back, "To hell with you!" No one had any energy to be in the victim condition, which had been so present before.

Dreamtime took over as we were transported for that brief period into another dimension. For that morning, in that room of one hundred and fifty people, we became a community, crying about, looking at, and laughing about our world, witnessing our tendency to dominate, to suffer, and to rebel. Nothing was solved immediately, but something moved, as the way people thought about war changed. Something irrational removed our national boundaries and brought us together. For that time and place, the spirits were exorcised, so to speak; there were no longer imperialists, terrorists, or victims. This was a beginning. It was both nothing and something.

Our future global village has a lot with which to deal. We will always need politicians, but we also need citizen-shaman-diplomats who deal with not only repressed gods, but dictators, victims, and minorities in a diverse world. What looks like trouble from one angle could be a new community from another.

In the past, whole communities dreamed together, circling and swaying as a unit as shamans took us dreaming with the ancestors. As you were healed, the whole culture gained access to the unknown and was revitalized. Cultures of the future will have to reinvent their own special methods of living with dreamtime if they are to survive. Each culture's methods will be different, but certain common elements can be predicted. People feel that life is worthwhile when they have participated in bringing up buried visions, forbidden spirits, and dead souls into their world. That is why dreaming together heals that eternal problem, feeling impotent about the direction of history.

The future city will be like the one you are in now, a place full of trouble, fun, and conflict. However, it might be different in one way from your present town. In this future city, you will no longer dream alone, because more people will be using altered states of consciousness, rather than gunpowder, to solve problems.

NOTES

CHAPTER 1. THE SHAMAN'S BODY

1. See bibliography for Eliade, *Archaic Techniques of Ecstasy*, and other authors, book titles, and details.

2. I am grateful to Castaneda for the developmental processes implied in his books—processes that many people go through as they develop shamanistic abilities related to living the dreaming-body. Though I am familiar with all of Castaneda's works, I draw mainly upon ideas from don Juan's first and most powerful lessons in *Teachings of don Juan, Separate Reality, Journey to Ixtlan, Tales of Power, Second Ring of Power*, and *Eagle's Gift*.

3. See especially Rinpoche, *Tibetan Book of Living and Dying*, and Evans-Wentz, *Tibetan Book of the Dead*.

4. Sutton et al., *Dreamings*.

5. Mander and Toms, in *Technology and Native Peoples,* discuss worldwide obliteration of native beliefs.

CHAPTER 3. THE PATH OF KNOWLEDGE

1. Eliade, *Shamanism, Archaic Techniques of Ecstasy,* 110.
2. Castaneda, *Separate Reality,* 213–14.
3. Sutton et al., *Dreamings,* 15.

CHAPTER 4. FIRST LESSONS

1. Sutton et al., *Dreamings,* 14.
2. Eliade, *Shamanism, Archaic Techniques of Ecstasy.*

CHAPTER 5. THE HUNTER

1. Castaneda, *Journey to Ixtlan,* 78.
2. Knudtson and Suzuki, in their wonderful book, *Wisdom of the Elders,* 102, describe how the Wintu Indians in northern California understand that some animals offer themselves to the hunter.

CHAPTER 6. THE WARRIOR

1. Eliade, *Shamanism, Archaic Techniques of Ecstasy,* 110.
2. Creation myths all deal with transcending the state of unconsciousness, symbolized by sleep, dreams, or the underworld. Sometimes, as in Castaneda's *Eagle's Gift,* 177, we find the transcendence symbolized in terms of living beyond life itself.
3. Castaneda, *Journey to Ixtlan,* 119.
4. Amy Mindell, "Moon in the Water," chap. 2.

CHAPTER 7. THE ALLY

1. Eliade, *Shamanism, Archaic Techniques of Ecstasy,* 91–92.
2. Ibid., 90.
3. Castaneda, *Journey to Ixtlan,* 61.
4. Ibid., 155.
5. Ibid., 206.

CHAPTER 8. THE ALLY'S SECRET

1. Castaneda, *Separate Reality,* 234.
2. Larousse, *Encyclopedia of Mythology,* 436–37.

3. Ibid., 437.

CHAPTER 9. THE DOUBLE

1. Castaneda, *Tales of Power,* 42–43.
2. Ibid., 76–77.
3. Ibid., 77–78.
4. Jung, *Memories, Dreams, Reflections,* 323.
5. Ibid., 324.

CHAPTER 10. THE PATH OF HEART

1. Castaneda, *Teachings of don Juan,* 106–7.
2. Castaneda, *Journey to Ixtlan,* 254.
3. Jung, *Memories, Dreams, Reflections,* 356.
4. Ibid.
5. Ibid.

CHAPTER 11. TRANSFORMATION AND SORCERY

1. Castaneda, *Journey to Ixtlan,* 216–17.

CHAPTER 12. DREAMING TOGETHER

1. Swan, *Sacred Places.*

CHAPTER 13. PHANTOMS AND REAL PEOPLE

1. Eliade discusses connections between modern India and aboriginal times, vestiges of the Austroasiatic civilization and pre-Aryan and pre-Dravidian peoples in *Yoga,* 344.

CHAPTER 14. THE DEATHWALK

1. Castaneda, *Tales of Power,* 283–84.
2. Ibid., 284ff.
3. Wotan is an archaic, German nature spirit—the "wild man" type.

CHAPTER 15. DREAMTIME AND CULTURAL CHANGE

1. See Neidhart, *Black Elk Speaks.*
2. Sutton et al., *Dreamings.*

BIBLIOGRAPHY

Castaneda, Carlos. *The Eagle's Gift.* New York: Simon & Schuster, 1985.

———. *Journey to Ixtlan: The Lessons of don Juan.* New York: Simon & Schuster, 1972.

———. *The Power of Silence.* New York: Simon & Schuster, 1988.

———. *The Second Ring of Power.* New York: Simon & Schuster, 1984.

———. *A Separate Reality: Further Conversations with don Juan.* New York: Simon & Schuster, 1971; Washington Square Press, 1991.

———. *Tales of Power.* New York: Simon & Schuster, 1974.

———. *The Teachings of don Juan: A Yaqui Way of Knowledge.* New York: Simon & Schuster, 1968; Washington Square Press, 1990.

Eliade, Mircea. *Shamanism, Archaic Techniques of Ecstasy.* Translated by Willard R. Trask. Princeton, NJ: Bollingen Foundation, Princeton Univ. Press, 1980.

———. *Yoga: Immortality and Freedom.* Translated by Willard R. Trask. London: Princeton-Bollingen paperback, 1970.

Evans-Wentz, ed. *The Tibetan Book of the Dead, or After-Death Experiences on the Bardo Plane.* New York: Oxford Univ. Press, 1960.

Feynman, Richard. "Space-Time Approach to Non Relativistic Quantum Mechanics." *Reviews of Modern Physics* (April 1948).

Halifax, Joan. *Shamanic Voices and the Shaman: The Wounded Healer.* New York: Dutton, 1979.

Harner, Michael. *The Way of the Shaman.* New York: Bantam Books, 1986.

Heinze, Ruth-Inge. *Shamans of the Twentieth Century.* New York: Irvington, 1991.

Houston, Jean. *The Possible Human: A Course in Extending Your Physical, Mental, and Creative Abilities.* Los Angeles: Jeremy Tarcher, 1982.

Ingerman, Sandra. *Soul Retrieval: Mending the Fragmented Self.* San Francisco: HarperSanFrancisco, 1991.

Jung, C. G. *Memories, Dreams, Reflections.* New York: Vintage Books, 1965, 1989.

———. *Mysterium Conjunctionis: Collected Works of C. G. Jung.* Edited by Sir Herbert Read, Michael Fordham, and Gerhard Adler. Translated by R. F. C. Hull. Princeton, NJ: Princeton Univ. Press (Bollingen Series XX, no. 12).

Larousse Encyclopedia of Mythology. Paul Hamlyn, 1969.

Mander, Jerry. *In the Absence of the Sacred.* New York: Sierra Club Books, 1991.

———. *Technologies and Native Peoples.* San Francisco: New Dimensions Radio, Audio Tape no. 2298, 1992.

Mindell, Amy. "Moon in the Water: The Metaskills of Process Oriented Psychology." Ph.D. diss., Union Institute, Cincinnati, OH, 1991.

Mindell, Arnold. *City Shadows, Psychological Interventions in Psychiatry.* New York and London: Viking-Penguin-Arkana, 1988.

———. *Coma, Key to Awakening: Working with the Dreambody Near Death.* Boston and London: Shambhala, 1989.

———. *Dreambody: The Body's Role in Revealing the Self.* Boston: Sigo Press, 1982; London: Viking-Penguin-Arkana, 1984.

———. *The Dreambody in Relationships.* New York and London: Viking-Penguin-Arkana, 1987.

———. *Inner Dreambodywork: Working on Yourself Alone.* New York and London: Viking-Penguin-Arkana, 1990.

———. *The Leader as Martial Artist, An Introduction to Deep Democracy: Techniques and Strategies for Resolving Conflict and Creating Community.* San Francisco: HarperSanFrancisco, 1992.

———. *River's Way: The Process Science of the Dreambody.* London and Boston: Viking-Penguin-Arkana, 1986.

———. *Working with the Dreaming Body.* London: Viking-Penguin-Arkana, 1984.

———. *The Year I: Global Process Work with Planetary Tensions.* New York and London: Viking-Penguin-Arkana, 1990.

———, with Amy Mindell. *Riding the Horse Backwards: Process Work in Theory and Practice.* New York and London: Viking-Penguin-Arkana, 1992.

Muktananda, Swami. *Play of Consciousness.* New York: SYDA Foundation, 1978.

Neidhardt, John G. *Black Elk Speaks: Being the Life Story of a Holy Man of the Oglala Sioux.* New York: Washington Square Press of Pocketbooks and Simon & Schuster, 1972.

Nicholson, Shirley, comp. *Shamanism: An Expanded View of Reality.* Wheaton, IL: The Theosophical Publishing House, 1987.

Rinpoche, Sogyal. *The Tibetan Book of Living and Dying.* San Francisco: HarperSanFrancisco, 1992.

Sutton, Peter, Christopher Anderson, Philip Jones, Francoise Dussart, and Steven Hemming, eds. *Dreamings: The Art of Aboriginal Australia.* New York: George Braziller, 1989.

Suzuki, David, and Peter Knudston. *The Wisdom of the Elders.* Toronto: Allen and Unwin, 1992.

Suzuki, Shunryu. *Zen Mind, Beginner's Mind: Informal Talks on Zen Meditation and Practice.* New York: Weatherhill, 1970.

Swan, James A. *Sacred Places.* Santa Fe, NM: Bear and Co., 1990.

Tart, Charles. *Waking Up.* Boston: Shambhala, 1987.

Toms, Michael. *Technologies and Native Peoples.* San Francisco: New Dimensions Radio, Audio Tape no. 2298, 1992.

Tzu, Lao. *Tao Te Ching: The Book of Meaning and Life.* Translated from the Chinese into German by Richard Wilhelm; translated into English by H. G. Ostwald. London and New York: Viking-Penguin-Arkana, 1985.

Walsh, Roger N. *The Spirit of Shamanism.* Los Angeles: Jeremy Tarcher, 1990.

INDEX

Australian aborigines (*continued*) 42, 213; native spirituality of, 42; on nature of power, 36; political reality of, 14

Average man, 77–78

Awareness: disciplined, 141; during healing ritual, 191; gaining and losing, 137–40; meaning of, 128; phases of development, 77–79

Barriers: fear as, 92–93, 188; lack of clarity as, 91–92; old age as a, 139; power as, 93–94

Beginner's mind, 69, 94

Black Elk, 213

Body: as ally, 103–7; connection between dreams and, 22–23; impact of wisdom on, 33; powers of the, 109–11; processing sensations of, 21–22. *See also* Dreamingbody

Bombay, 175–78

Book of the Dead (Buddhist Tibetan), 10, 156

Book of the Dead (Egyptian), 156

Buddha, 207

Buddhism: achieving processwork goal, 35; on impermanence of life, 48; processes of personal growth, 32; on sense of identity, 10; strengths of, 12

Bush soul, 95

Cabalistic Judaism, 32

Caelum, 44

Callings, 5

Castaneda, Carlos: apprenticeship of, 60; attracted to devil's weed, 99; challenged by woman apprentice, 165–66; *Eagle's Gift,* 35; finds "place of power," 58; lack of responsibility of, 52;

observes Genaro, 131; on self-identification, 5; tested by Mescalito, 76; uses fantasies to call up images, 125–26

Change. *See* Processwork

Chi, 63

Clarity, 91–92

Coma, Key to Awakening (Mindell), 95, 112

Community. *See* Groups

Compassion, 85, 100

Conflict: dreaming to heal, 211–12; as fate of warrior, 200–202; shamanism impact on, 217–19

Controlled abandonment: described, 157–60; practicing, 160–61

Courage, 142

Death: dreamingbody continues past, 107; dreamingbody during process of, 133–34; experience of near-, 24, 95, 96; fantasy, 50–52, 54–55; freedom through, 162–63; the last dance and, 111–13; modern rejection of, 156–57; Tibetan spirituality regarding, 112

Deathwalk: beginning the, 200–202; defining, 199–200; exercises, 208–9; the groups response to, 202–4; length of life, 207–8; surviving the, 204–7. *See also* The Warrior

Depression: disguised as detachment, 94–95; phantoms and, 192

Detachment: depression disguised as, 94–95; from paths, 142–43; from personal history, 46–50, 55, 147–48; heartfulness, 85; little smoke experiences and, 99

Devil's weed: power of, 98–99; use of, 99–102

ARNOLD MINDELL

Discipline, 140–41

Dismemberment rituals, 48

Don Juan: ally of, 98; compares hunters and warriors, 77; concepts of warrior and the double, 8; on dangers of sorcery, 37; on deathwalk survival, 204; detachment of, 49–50; on developing a double, 134; on devil's weed, 98–99; on facing the ally, 114; on gaining personal power, 153; on Genaro's double, 126; on hunter's training, 62, 63; on importance of group, 166; on the last dance, 111–12; on living environment, 41, 43; method of instruction of, 9–10; names the barriers, 91; on path of heart, 139–40; personal development stages, 28; on personal power, 105; on phantoms, 37; on phases of development, 77–78; on responsibility, 52; retells eagle's gift, 35; on returning to reality, 196; on self-identification, 5, 181; on stepping out of time, 130; teaches how to dream, 81; tests Castaneda, 76

Double, The: described, 125–28; developing your, 129–30, 134; exercises, 136; Jung's encounter with, 135–36. *See also* Secondary processes

Double signals: described, 25–27; power traced through, 65; recognizing, 128; repressing, 127

Dreambody: The body's Role in Revealing the Self (Mindell), 16

Dreambody, 22

Dreambody, The (Mindell), 183

Dreambody in Relationships, The (Mindell), 16

Dreamfields: defining, 129; phantom, 201; within large groups, 133

Dreamingbody: continues past death, 107; described, 3–5; experience while dying, 133–34; experience within, 131; health benefits of, 19–20, 60; manifested by "shadow," 38–39; processing, 21–23; requirements of the, 153–54; shaman's ability to follow, 58; Taoism development of, 32. *See also* Shaman's body

Dreamings: Australian aboriginal, 11, 13, 42; by a double, 134–36; calls to Shamanism through, 9; dangers of learning to, 81; metaskills of, 85–90; as route to power, 79–85; as social activism, 212; special tasks during, 84

Dream maker, 23

Dreams: appearance of allies in, 97; as body snapshots, 20–21; interpretation of, 76–77; learning to have, 83; measuring growth through, 73–74; projecting images within, 128–29. *See also* Fantasies

Dreamtime, 23

Drugs: alcohol, 114, 213; power induced by, 98–99, 114; seeking altered consciousness through, 9, 96. *See also* Hallucinations

Eagle's Gift (Castaneda), 35

Edges: clarity, 91–92; fear, 92–93; power, 93–94

Eliade, Mircea: on callings, 5; on shaman's path, 35; on stages of becoming shaman, 28; on the warrior's ally, 95

Enlightenment: Western psychotherapy, 32–33; Zen, 32

THE SHAMAN'S BODY   231

Environment: body powers part of, 109–10; dangers to the, 28–29; shamanism on, 41–46. *See also* Nature

Familiars. *See* The Ally
Fantasies: appearance of allies in, 97; Castaneda uses, 125–26; death, 50–52, 54–56; experiencing, 64–66; patterns of, 87. *See also* Dreams
Fear, 92–93, 188
Feynman, Richard, 131–32
Field. *See* Dreamfields
Fire ritual, 45–46
First attention, 23–25
Freudian psychoanalysts, 32
Fukushima, Keido, 32, 69

Gaia, 174
Gait of power, 105–6
Gandhi, 207
Genaro: on deathwalk survival, 204; double of, 126–27; stepping out of time, 130–31; on tasks, 199
Gestalt psychology, 12
Gestalt therapy, 32
Groups: exercises, 178–79; laws of the inner and outer, 200–202; pain sharing with, 170–76; ritual by Kenyan community, 167–70; rule enforcement by, 202–4; shamanism impact on, 215–19; viewpoint of large, 190–91; warrior clans, 165–67
Gurus, 184–86. *See also* Teachers

Hallucinations: ally appearance through, 104; dreaming process during, 25; experiencing, 64. *See also* Drugs

Hannah, Barbara, 101
Healers: on cause of illness, 215; detachment of African, 49; Girami, 92; Jesus Christ as, 97; shaman's ability as, 58–59
Healing: dreambody viewpoint on, 110; finding right spot of, 58–60; powerbody for, 103–7; rituals, 214; shamanic approach to, 191
Healing hands, 109
Hiawatha, 206
Homosexuals, 173–74
Hopi Indians, 43
Humanistic psychology, 12
Humility: changing through, 100–101; importance of, 74, 75
Hunter, The: attentions described, 28, 83; character described, 78; commitment to shamanism, 60–62; dangers of personal history, 67–70; exercises for, 70–71; shamanistic testing, 58–60; training steps of, 62–67; vs. the warriors, 77, 95. *See also* Prey

I Ching: consulting, 57; on the spirit, 70; use of divination, 12
Identity: detachment of personal history, 46–50; maturation of, 34; path of heart's lack of, 142–43; retained during dreaming, 84–85; spirit determines, 5, 181; spirit vs. self-, 69–70; transformation of, 5–6, 10–11, 123–28. *See also* Personal growth
Illness, 215. *See also* Healing
Indigenous culture: alcoholism within, 114; breaking apart of, 166; connection with nature, 44–45; dreamingbody